MW00955476

Congratulations in taking the first step in starting your own company. You join millions of individuals who have decided to take their future into their own hands and accept the challenge of starting down a path of personal satisfaction and financial benefits. There will be challenges you will overcome, there will be new business relationship you will develop, there will be moments of discouragement but there will be no greater satisfaction than being your own boss and controlling your own future.

What qualifies me to guide you down this path of starting and maintaining your new business? As with many things in life I stumbled into this field after a small business I was managing was transferred to a new owner. The new owner used me for a few years then decided that they had the skills and were ready to manage their business. Now being unemployed after moving into a new house with my wife and three children the financial pressure mounted. I was approached by a friend to join him in his courier service. After 15 years of being involved in this service I have acquired the knowledge, skills and understanding of what it takes to start and maintain a courier service. These 15 years have been great! I have had the pleasure of satisfying hundreds of customers from delivering a monthly envelope to multi-million dollars a year banking contract.

There are numerous companies in the need of having items pick up and delivered throughout the United States. These companies are looking for a service that they can trust with their items and their customer's items. As you unfold and read the pages in this book you will be amazed at all the businesses who use courier service. And as you begin to reach out into the business world you will be overwhelm with how much business there is for you to grow into.

How to use this Book

This book was designed to be easy to read and easy to implement. It provides you with all the information you need to get started immediately. Wisdom dictates that you start off slowly and comfortably. It will not be fair to you, your family nor to your customers that you bit off more business then you can handle. Trust me, in due time you will be on your way to business and personal success if you follow all the information provided for you in this book.

DO NOT try to learn all of this information at once nor try to have a complete understanding of the courier service business before venturing out and starting your company. It is suggested that you read though this material once then start your own business. However, if you can't wait to start your own business jump out there and get started. Not knowing your personality or your business experience this book contains information in areas of business etiquette, marketing, time management, contact management, useful technologies, business development, legal issues, business contracts, insurance cost and concerns, financial management along with personal and business management as they pertain to owning and managing a courier company.

Keep this book with you during the first few weeks of starting your business; refer to it whenever you have an issue that you need to review. And during down time consider rereading a particular chapter. As you read this book your mind will begin to translate this information into your own ideas and practices. Taking notes as you read this manual will strengthen your ability to retain the information and transform this information into your own personal style of business growth and management.

The margins are wide in order for you to have room to make your own personal notes. Write whatever enters your mind as you read this book. May my thoughts spark your thoughts!

Table of Content

Chapter 1

Reasons to Start and Own a Courier Service

Each of us desires to earn an income that will supply our family with food, clothing and shelter. Our culture also expects us to be able to have more then what we need to care for ourselves and for others. This desire to earn income can be achieved through providing a service or selling a product. Owning your own business gives you the ability to provide a healthy living and achieve personal fulfillment. So why start a courier service as a source of income and fulfillment? There are several reasons:

1. Low startup cost. Starting a business can be costly. The goal in starting a company is to do so without acquiring too much debt. The startup cost for a courier company can range from a few hundred dollars to a couple thousand. The cost depends on what you currently have. Most people have a car, a cell phone and some ability to work without a source of financial income for a few weeks while waiting for the customer to pay for the service provided.

2. A needed & niche service. In this high tech world of computers, faxes, emails and the ability to transfer loads of data via the internet, businesses still need items moved from one location to another. You will be pleasantly surprise to find out just how many businesses use courier services. More about specific business needs later in this book, but for the moment, just think of all the U.S. Postal Service, Federal Express, UPS and the like whose sole purpose is to pick up items and deliver them. There are plenty of companies and businesses who need local courier service.

It will not be difficult for you to find your niche. All you need to do is figure out how you can do the work better than your competition. Once again this topic will be discussed later in this book. But for the moment all you need to understand is that you can and will find a niche that will provide financial and personal success.

3. Personal growth. Not knowing where you are in life I can only assume you are ready for a change and a challenge. Starting, owning and managing a courier company has immense potential personal growth which is only limited by your personal desire. You have no limits except for those you impose upon yourself. With this in mind you can understand that owning your own courier service will have challenges and risk, but the information you find in this book will eliminate many challenges and reduce your risk.

4. Freedom with your time, schedule and personal life. We all want a certain amount of freedom. Some more than others and those who want more understand that there is a tradeoff between spending long hours working for someone else who sits back and reaps the benefit of your labors or spending long hours working for ourselves and reaping the benefit of our own labors. If you worked for someone else you know what I mean. Working for someone else ends up being less than gratifying. There is no sweeter reward then having control over your own time, schedule, and personal life. You pick the hours you want to work. You pick the work you want to do. You pick when you want to go on a three day vacation or spend a month exploring that foreign country you longed to travel too. Having your own courier company provides you with freedom and flexibility.

5. Financial payoff. There is good financial payoff in the courier service. But you must be wise in starting and managing your new business venture in order to receive the highest financial payoff. Generally speaking the higher the business risk the higher the financial payoff. The goal in providing you with this information is to equip you to lower your risk and increase your financial payoff. How much money can you expect during your first few years in the courier business? I can comfortable say you can make at least $20,000 a year working part time and at least $50,000 a year working full time. But I will not be surprised that there will be those who will achieve a six figure income within three to four years. The business is out there all you need to do is go get it.

6. Tax benefits. There is a tax benefit to owning your own courier company. Tax laws are always changing so it's important that you review your financial information with you accountant (and yes you will want to hire an accountant). The best tax advantage is the mileage deduction you receive from the moment you leave your house to the time you return back to your house. I know of one driver who was able to receive a larger tax deduction then his income. This may sound odd but it's true and he had the documents to prove it. Even if you have a part time courier service all cost to register and insure your vehicle is a tax deduction. Anything you purchase for yourself that pertains to your business is also a tax deduction. Keep a record of all your purchases.

As you see there are several outstanding reasons to start and own a courier company. As time progresses, you will come to the understanding that you have made the right decision in venturing in your own business. The risk will be minimal, the rewards outstanding. I have named only a few reasons to start and own a courier service. As the weeks months and years pass you will formulate your own healthy reasons why you enjoy the work that you do.

Chapter 2

Getting started in the Courier Service industry

You have this book and you want to start your own courier service business immediately. This is what you are to do and why you should do it immediately.

How…Start working for a courier service as an independent subcontractor while you are working thru this book.

Why…by starting your company now your will

- Start the cash flow to bootstrap your business. Learn what bootstrapping is in chapter 4. - Apply what you're learning in this book.
- Learning what it's like to work as a subcontractor will give you a better understanding of what is required when you start hiring your own subcontractors.

Where to look…to find a job as an independent subcontractor

- Local newspapers is where some courier companies advertise their need to hire drivers.
- The Phone book is another source for locating courier companies. Keep in mind many courier companies desire to have a low profile and don't list their business in the phone directory, but look any way because those who do list will have a strong customer base.   - Internet searches are perhaps the best way to locate a courier company in your area. Websites like Craig's List and jobs.com are also a place where you will find companies hiring independent subcontractors.

How to get hired…

- Call the courier service company and ask to speak to the Operations Manager.

- Ask what type of courier work they do. Read the chapter on types of courier runs to give you an understanding of what type of work they are discussing. Some courier companies exclusively commit themselves to only doing one style of courier runs. Some only do one up work while others only do mail runs. By the way, it will be in your best profit line that you offer various types of courier service and not become exclusive. Once your company is up and running with steam.

- Let them know you are interested. Tell them what type of vehicle you have and what type of work you're interested in doing.

Do the work right & start your business with good habits…

- Be on time
- Develop a good attitude
- Keep your eyes and ears wide open to opportunities
- Practice what you are learning thru this book

Keep a log of all your activities…

- Mileage: before you leave the driveway of your home, record the mileage odometer number and when you drive back home at the end of your day's work, record the number…this is important information for your tax records. Keep this information in a mileage log or notebook.

   - Expenses: record all that you spend money on to perform your subcontracting duties. Keep all receipts and log them into an expense notebook. This also is important information for your tax records.
- Directions: keep a notebook of all directions given to you.
- Customers: who are you picking up work from and who are you delivering too. Record their name, business name, address and contact information. Later in this book you will learn why this information is important.

- Get the name and numbers of your fellow workers, or in this case, your fellow independent subcontractors. Remember their names and cell number. As your business grows you may want to hire some of them to do work for you.

Now that you are working as a subcontractor for another courier service take what you are learning and work thru this manual. As you begin to apply the information in this book you will see all the possibilities of your potential business growth. Step-by-step you will become a successful business owner.

Since you are a subcontractor you need to honor any written agreement you commit yourself too. That may include a certain amount of insurance coverage, dress code, confidentiality agreements and non-competition clauses. Make sure this agreement does not limit you from doing work for yourself or other courier companies. If so, you will need to review your commitment with this company when the time comes. Keep silent about your intentions of branching out on your own while doing work for another courier company. This will cause unneeded stress on your relationship with them causing them to think that you are there to steal away their customers. There is plenty of work out there and there are no reasons for you to steal away customers with whom you have enter into an agreement. This book will teach you how to get your own customers without stealing from the company who hired you as a subcontractor. You would not like it if one of your subcontractor tries to steal away our customer so don't try to steal away customers from the company who hired you and with whom you have entered into an agreement.

Once you gain an understanding of how the courier service industry operates through the experience you gain, use this book to set out on your own.

Chapter 3

Naming your Courier Service

Naming your business appropriately is vital in communicating to your customers who you are and what you do. There are a few basic rules to follow when naming your courier service. Have fun developing a good name and by all means, once you have settled on several potential names, get the opinion of others. Ask family members or friends for their help in considering which name is the best.

Naming Tips:

1) Keep the name short and simple. Try not using more than three to four words in your name and each word should be one to three syllables. Keeping the name short will make it easier for your customers to remember.

2) The name should be easy to pronounce, easy to read and understandable. The easier you make your name to roll off the lips of your staff and customers the better it will be for them and for you. Don't use a name that uses words that are spelled differently than how the words sound. This causes confusion.

3) Avoid using your personal name. There may come a time when you desire to sell your business and having your personal name attached will decrease the value of the sale. However, if you desire to have your personal name attached to your business as a means of insuring quality service by all means do it. The choice is yours.

4) Your name should reflect the type of service you will be doing. Examples are 'courier service' or 'express service' in your business name. This tells your potential customers what you are all about. Allow your name to describe your service. However, keep in mind that you will be expanding your courier service into other related activities, including warehousing (we will get to that later). When you venture into other related services then you can add that service to your name or simply start the related service with a new name.

5) Don't limit your courier service by naming it with only one aspect of the courier industry. If you use a name that only reflects a portion of the courier service industry then you are limiting the growth of your business. For example, if you start your company doing medical transport and you name your company 'Express Medical Transport' then you are limiting your ability to reach other areas of the courier industry like…banking or data processing to potential new customers.

6) Don't name your business according to geographical location. This will limit the expansion of your business into other geographical areas.

7) The name is to be distinctive. Does your name set you apart from your competitors?

8) Is the name marketable? If a potential customer web searches a courier service you need to insure that your name will add to your market appeal. Market appeal will include the visual appeal. Does it look good in print for web sites, publications, advertisements etc? Also consider the abbreviations of the name, making sure that the initials don't spell something offensive.

9) Consider using a Tag-line. A Tag-line is a concise phrase that depicts the focus of how you conduct your business. The Tag-line is not to be part of your name but a quick, catchy phrase that you can add to your business cards or other advertisements.

Registration of your business name:

1) Register your name with the correct State agency. Each State has different requirements to register a fictitious business name. A business name which is not named in your own personal name is referred to as an assumed, fictitious name or 'Doing Business As' (DOA) title. In order for States to manage fictitious business names many require the fictitious name to be registered by State or county. This web link will instruct you in your residing State. The cost for registration is

minimal and is required in order for you to open a business bank account.
http://www.business.gov/register/business-name/dba.html

2) Do a web searches to see if the name you chose is being used by another business. Be careful of copy right and trade name infringements. Registration of your name will protect you from others using your business name and causing confusion.

Chapter 4

Bootstrapping – How to finance your startup cost!

What is Bootstrapping? – Bootstrapping is starting and growing your own business by doing everything yourself including the financing. So as you can well see the idea of bootstrapping is two concepts wrapped into one word. The first concept is 'who does all the work?' The second concept is 'where do I get the startup money?'

Do all the work yourself - this is a great way for you to start your business, even if it means a slower start to the business. This does not mean you don't get some help along the way but what it does mean is that you are responsible for what gets done and what does not get done. You set the dream, you set the direction, you set the pace, you set how much work gets done, you set the plan of action and you do all the work. Sounds like fun!!!! And fun is what it is all about…keep the right attitude and it will all work out.

Keep in mind that you are responsible for all advertising, marketing, sales, phone calls, appointments, time management, accounting/bookkeeping, profit-loss statements, banking, accounts payable, accounts receivable, business registration, research, hiring employees and subcontractors, networking, customer service, local regulations and anything else that needs to be done and get done. It's gonna be great!

The advantage to this method of starting your business is that you will learn all aspects of your business. Some things will come natural to you and other things will be a challenge but you will have an understanding of how you and your business will operate on the road to success. You also will have deep satisfaction knowing that you are in control of your own future. You may have moments of despair and dark feelings but pull yourself up from your bootstraps and get to work.

Please, you don't have to do all the work all at once. You will do your research (this book) and take one piece of the grand puzzle at a time. Step by step you will grow into your business and before you know it you will be a 'jack of all trade' when it comes to your new business. Once you have a handle on all aspects of your business you are ready to consider where you need help and who to hire to assist you. You have natural gifts, abilities and skills that you will gravitate towards. That's good! You also have areas of business you will not like nor be very good at performing or achieving. That's good! Look at all you do well and don't do well as insight into how you can best achieve what you desire.

Finance the business yourself - this is also a great way for you to start your business, even if it means a slower start to the business. The biggest advantage to starting this way is that in the long run you will have a larger profitability because you will not have any debt payments to banks or other money lending institutions. You will be relying on savings, early cash flow, sweat equity and cost cuttings to fund your start up courier service.

Here are some principles and suggestions you need to understand that will assist you to bootstrapping your finances.

~ Shrink your spending – this means personal and professional spending. Remember this phrase: Short term pain, long term gain. You need to learn how to live without. Without what you ask? Learn how to live without the luxuries of our American culture. Most Americans begin to cry foul when things we take for granted are taken away from us. So you are going to have to learn to give up anything that's going to cost you money. Magazine subscriptions, eating out at fancy restaurants, smoking and alcohol, going to the movies, etc…

This also applies to your business spending as well. We all want to start our business with a high tech smart phone and we can justify the reasons why. Instead buy a regular inexpensive cell phone with basic coverage. The time will come when you will be ready for that latest and greatest smart phone and that time will be when your cash flow says you can afford it. Apply this principle to everything you are considering to purchase.

~ Get that first customer fast – Get off the couch and go get that first customer. You have all the tools and know how right in front of you. Don't think you have to be an expert in the courier service before you get your first customer. Nor think that you have to read this whole book before you get that first customer. The quicker you get the cash flowing the better you will feel about yourself and your new venture.

~ Focus on cash flow – when you first start your business your mind will beginning running in all sorts of different directions. You will need to be mindful of all aspects but you need to focus on cash flow. Get the customer, do the work, bill the customer, cash the check. This is the cycle that needs the most attention so focus.

~ Postpone profit in exchange for growth – as the cash begins to flow into the business you will be tempted to take some for yourself but hold back. It will be worth it in the long run. Reinvest that money back into the business. Use it for growth like getting more customers into your cash flow cycle.

~ Expect challenges – don't think it's going to be a road paved with gold. You have your work cut out for you and you will have your challenges. The key is to be prepared for them as much as you can be. This includes starting with adjusting to the right attitude. You may want to review the chapter on self-management every once in a while. Challenges are going to come and you are the one who is to rule over those challenges. Don't sit back and be knocked down nor knocked around by discouraging situations, competition, slow progress or insufficient knowledge or skill. Pick yourself up by the 'bootstraps' and get moving.

~ Pick your battles – At times you will be overwhelm with all the activities that go into starting your own business. Don't fight on all fronts at the same time nor think that you have to because you will not have time, energy or finances to fight all those battles at once. Pick the right battles. Prioritize them and always keep your focus on the cash flow cycle.

~ Always think, 'How can I do this better' – be a firm believer in improvement. Become known for simplifying a business plan, course of action or utilizing technology and individuals to improve the function and form of business dealings. Improvement on the thoughts you find in this book. Make it work for you to make your life easier, better and more profitable.

Bootstrapping your business can be fun, exciting and challenging. It is low risk with high rewards. You will need to do some thinking, than more thinking about how you approach life and the world around you. Your attitude will improve and become more conscience of all that you do because it will affect how successful you will become. As you look back on this time you will be amazed at how you have grown and smile at all that you have accomplished.

Chapter 5

Different types of courier routes

There are different types of routes (runs) that you will be asked to do. Becoming familiar with the different types of routes will assist you in asking the right questions when it comes to getting details of how to best serve your customers. This knowledge will also help you in knowing what to charge for the runs and how to billing your customers. Terminology varies from one company to another but here is a basic breakdown of various routes or runs.

Regular daily routes – this will become your bread and butter. These are the routes that offer you constant, steady and profitable work. What I call regular daily routes are routes that you do Monday through Friday during normal business hours. These routes offer you a ready understanding of what you're going to do when you wake up each morning. As you begin to grow your business these are the routes that you will give to your independent subcontractors, because they are easier to hand off to someone else and easier to manage.

Weekly routes – these routes are done perhaps once or twice a week. For example if you do work for a payroll company they may have you picked up paperwork on one day then deliver the payroll checks on the following day. It is always nice when you are able to include these deliveries into your regular daily routes.

Monthly routes – these are routes that have monthly pickup and deliveries. Usually you will know it well in advance when these deliveries need to be made. Often you're given plenty of time to think through how you will make the deliveries.

Occasional runs – occasional routes are those routes that your customers, from time to time, may need you to do for them that is not part of a regular route or part of their regular routine but instead are done on an as needed bases. Usually these are last-minute pickups or deliveries that your customer will need to have done.

For example, I had one customer who called me once a year to deliver accounting records during the month of January.

One ups – As your business begins to grow and expand you will find that there are customers who need what is known as one up work. This work is basically picked up at a location and delivered to another location and timing is not consistent. Often these routes are done as emergencies. They can be as small as a letter from one end of town to the other or picking up multiple boxes and delivering them to another state. It is very important for you to do these 'one up' jobs, because they offer you the opportunity to demonstrate your ability to a new customer. However, do not sacrifice your regular daily routes to do 'one up' jobs, if you find yourself in a position of having to be forced to choose. As soon as you are able to consider having a family member, friend or another subcontracting courier with whom you have developed a relationship to assist you when you have one up work offered to you. There are some courier companies who only do 'one up' jobs. One up work offers a higher level of income because is often done on a last-minute basis but the sacrifice is that there is no steady stream of work or income.

Round trips – these are runs that you will pick up at one location, deliver it, then return a different package or document back to original location. How you want to bill your customer on these routes depends on whether they are regular routes or emergency routes. Generally speaking the return trips are calculated at a rate that is 50% to 75% of the one way trip.

Hooks – these are runs that do pick-ups or deliveries which are tacked on to a current already existing route. For example you have customer who wants you to make a delivery from point A to point B but they also have a pickup at point B and they would like for you to deliver to point C. Depending on where point C is in your route you can offer your customer a lower price for the hook run. How these runs become profitable is when you are able to take a package from a customer and hook it onto another run of another customer. You are able to charge a full rate to the second customer. You have greater flexibility when it comes to pricing out hook runs. The goal is to satisfy your customers and increase your profits. Hooks are good for providing both.

The runs listed above are style or types of runs. The following are runs based on time. Because of the nature of different runs you will need to learn how to set and adjust different prices for the various styles and timing. After a while you will be able to do to ask the right questions of your customer and calculate prices quickly.

Same day deliveries – are generally for high value items often used by the legal, banking, data processing and the medical industries. Because the deliveries are time sensitive the pricing is usually set fairly high but the price will vary depending on the time parameters and what is being delivered. These are deliveries that are usually given to one driver without handing it off to another driver. A dedicated run is the industry term for packages that need to be done ASAP, without combining packages from another customer.

Emergency or rush deliveries - sometimes you receive a call from a customer who is going basically want you to drop everything and make a delivery. These are what we call emergency runs. An example is delivering for a payroll company who forgot to place a particular payroll check into the regular batch of checks. Therefore this one check needs to be rushed to the recipient. They will ask you to pick up the check and deliver as quickly as possible. These runs offer you an opportunity to charge the customer more money than what you would charge for a regular daily route. This will be your highest priced delivery.

Overnight deliveries – these are deliveries that often are picked up one day, taken back to office or warehouse, sorted then loaded onto a different driver's route. Special security measures need to be set to insure that contents are safe overnight and the paperwork involved needs to reflect signatures between the various drivers.

There are courier companies who only specialize in one style of runs. They market and promote themselves to that single style. I encourage you to be flexible and provide the type of services that your customers need. As you market your services and you are given the chance to do a new style of run that you are not accustom too, figure out a way to do the run or runs. This will promote growth and profitability.

Chapter 6

Who Uses Courier Service?

There are thousands of individuals, businesses and companies who need and use courier service. At first it may seem that you will only be able to find a few customers but the following list will give you a greater understanding of where you can find good customers to grow your business.

Lawyers ~ Lawyers use courier service for various reasons which makes marketing to them valuable. Court files, documents sent and received from their clients and often for emergence services. The profit from lawyers is best gain when you are able to service a group of lawyers and you can overlap your energy. You will often find that lawyers gather in office clusters. Use this to your advantage. Also, as is the nature of lawyers, they talk to one another and word will spread of your abilities and service. Once you begin to enter into public court houses to file documents for lawyers any additional lawyer you add as a customer will increase your profit. At first, because of competition, your profits will be low but as always, outstanding service always stands out. Lawyers also need rushed documents that need to be signed by their clients. This type of work is more profitable so if you build a strong client base your efforts will be rewarded.

Data processing companies ~ Data processing companies are great clients to have because they will require daily, weekly, monthly and emergence service. I recommend you first market data processing companies because of the regular routine of courier needs they have. You will be picking up paperwork documents from their customer, deliver to the data processing company, who then will usually transfer the paper documents into electronic information. This electronic information will be sent back to their customer via electronic service but more likely on disks, CD's or DVD's. Also, their customers will want the original paperwork to be delivered back. Examples are medical records, coupons for mailing service, billing or any other service that requires transferring information from paper to electronic.

There are data processing companies all over the United States. Many cities and towns have three to a dozen data processing companies. It's simply mind-boggling. All you need to do is open up your Yellow Pages and look under data processing and you'll be amazed by the number of data processing companies in your area. All of these companies utilize courier service.

Banks ~ Banks have undergone a transformation in order to fulfill the Federal Reserve's demands. At one point when a bank customer would take a check into a bank or into a retail store the physical check would have to go to the Federal Reserve in order to be processed. But 'Check 21' has changed that requirement. Now the Federal Reserve is demanding that banks send the check information to them electronically. This has been a difficult decision for courier companies. However, there are still two areas where banks use courier service. One area is inter-office mail. When the bank has several branch locations there are loans, documents and other paperwork that needs to be moved from the administration office to the various branches and vise verse. It is in the banks best interest to have this done daily and at a regular time. Another area of service is having their checks delivered to a check processing center. Many banks will have the physical check taken to a clearing house and the clearing house will scan the checks, format them and send the information to the Federal Reserve on behalf of the banks. Another service banks are offering to their business account holder is to pick up their daily bank deposits. Basically the bank will contract a courier service to go to the business and pick up the deposits and take them to bank branch and make deposit. This is often a daily service the business would like to have done because the bank will make the funds available usually within 24 hours.

Medical facilities ~ small private medical practices to large hospitals with various office locations utilize courier service. Several suggestions for you to market are:

~ MRI centers. Often they have outsourced their films to be read by doctors in other locations and hire courier companies to make the pick-ups and deliveries. Depending on the size of the facility and patient count you may be needed to do several daily trips.

~Dental services - I did work for a small company who would make teeth implants and dentures. I would pick up the teeth and deliver them to local dentist.

~Blood banks - during blood drives the blood needs to be picked up several times a day and taken to the blood bank. Also, blood needs to be taken from the blood bank to local hospitals.

~ Hospitals. The best hospitals are those who have satellite locations. There is a hospital that I have served who had several clinics throughout their county. Primarily the work is transporting x-rays, MRI scans, medical records, occasionally computers, medical equipment and even patients.

~Medical equipment & supplies. There are numerous medical supplies companies both retail and wholesale which need courier and delivery services. This is often emergency courier service and therefore a higher billable. Do not overlook hospice care organizations, physical therapy offices and medical transcriptions.

Do not overlook any medical profession. It's very important to keep in mind that medical records have strict privacy enforcement. You will have to sign a confidentiality agreement when transporting medical documentations which have strict governmental oversight regulations that the medical profession need to adhere too.

Port services ~ there are thousands of international shipments coming and going throughout the nation. With each of these shipments there is massive amount of documentation associated with each import and export. This documentation is often handled by brokers who are hired by the companies who need items shipped between ports. This paperwork needs to be in proper order and timely delivered. Shipping brokers are protective with their work and customer base and they often have a close tie with other brokers, almost like a brotherhood. The service you can provide is picking up paperwork at a port (airports and seaports), then taking paperwork to broker who then reviews the documentation, and then it gets sent to the Customs House. At the Customs House the paperwork is time stamped and processed. Once processed it gets delivered back to shipping broker. This whole process usually takes a few days to a week. However, with all the shipments coming and going in and out of the nation, you potentially will be making several round trips several times a day.

SPECIAL NOTE*: In order for you to enter a port you must have Transportation Worker Identification Credential, also known as a TWIC card. This card is inexpensive and easy to acquire. All you need to do is go on to the Transportation Security Administration website and provide the needed information. At this time the card takes about 6 to 8 weeks to process, cost $132.50 and is valid for 5 years.*

Getting the door open for doing work for Customs brokers is difficult but well worth the energy because once you do work for one company other companies will become available to you. The beauty is that you are already going to the same location for the second, third and fourth broker as you are for the first broker. This means profit, profit, profit.

If you live near a seaport or airport (international, national and regional) then venture into this type of courier service. Just open up the yellow pages or search the internet and locate shipping brokers in your area. This type of business alone can keep you and several workers busy throughout the day and weeks. This is great work if you live along the coastal areas of our country where there are shipping ports within a day's drive from one another, because a Customs Broker will have offices located in those port cities. At first you can approach them about making pick-ups and deliveries between their offices. For example, Jersey City to Philadelphia; Philadelphia to Baltimore; Baltimore to Newport; San Francisco to San Diego or up and down the Mississippi River to only name a few port cities near one another.

Advertisers ~ the advertising industry uses all sorts of computer technologies that have advanced the ability to communicate effectively. But when they need to get 'hard copies' into the hands of their customers they use courier companies. Their use of couriers is often sporadic. However, do not neglect approaching advertising agencies because they get you into other businesses that will allow you to expand your customer base. Always have a smile on your face and a business card ready when you make a delivery for advertisers.

 Printing companies ~ the work you can do for a printing company will vary. Many printing companies have their own vans and even trucks to make deliveries. However, they also use courier companies to handle smaller deliveries. As your business grows you may want to consider buying a van or at least rent a van for making deliveries for printing companies.

Pharmaceutical warehouses ~ pharmaceutical companies contract their delivery service to large distribution companies. These companies are often low profile, using unmarked warehouses and unmarked vehicles to lower any unwanted attraction. Many of these warehouses receive tractor trailers during the night, sort out cartons full of drugs in the morning then divide the deliveries according to a designate route. These designate routes are subcontracted out to independent subcontractors who made the delivery from the warehouse to local drug stores and hospitals. Along this same line of work, drug stores are also delivering drugs and supplies to their customer's homes. Controlled substances require additional attention such as special documentation, temperature control or unique security procedures. Make sure you understand what the pharmaceutical special requirements are before you start doing work for them.

Auto parts warehouses ~ this type of delivery is similar to pharmaceutical warehouses. With the exception that subcontractors do not get a designate route. Instead, drivers wait until a retail store, a dealership or a local mechanic calls in an order. The deliveries are made according to how many stores need deliveries. Often a driver will know where the stores are located and design his own route that is cost effective.

Office supply warehouses ~ this work is also similar to pharmaceutical warehouses and auto parts warehouses. Perhaps the biggest difference is that office supply warehouses use small box trucks and vans to make deliveries of office furniture and large boxes of assorted products. However, they also use subcontractors to make daily routed deliveries to small office supply retail store and even home deliveries. Because of the 'I got to have it now syndrome' many office supply warehouses use subcontractors for emergency deliveries.

Payroll companies ~ payroll outsourcing was accept in many large companies during the 1990's. The concept of outsourcing has changed over the years but the use of outsourcing payroll still exists. Small and medium size businesses gather payroll information then transmit that information via computers to a payroll company. The following day checks are printed and need delivering. This work is often done early in the morning which is great for those who enjoy driving during low traffic patterns.

Mail fulfillment companies ~ there are many businesses that use fulfillment companies to handle various projects. These projects include mailing advertisements to specific potential customers or zip code specific areas. Another project that fulfillment companies offer is organizing customer surveying information. This includes fact gathering to target potential customers for their customers. The type of projects they offer really does not concern you but what does concern you is your business growth. These mail fulfillment companies need and use courier services to pick up and deliver to various post offices and businesses. The service you provide will depend on the amount of volume the fulfillment companies need to have picked up or delivered. For instance, I had a mail fulfillment company which used my services once a month to deliver several trays of mail advertisement to a post office in a different city. I also did work for a fulfillment company who had several van loads of mail trays picked up three to four times a day. As you see this type of work can vary but your goal is to provide a needed service no matter what the volume or timing.

Parts manufactures ~ there are companies, often found in industrial parks that manufacture various parts. Parts like hydraulic hoses, refrigeration parts, industrial air conditioning parts & computer parts to only name a few. These parts need to get into the hands of their customer quickly, often to handle an emergence situation. Let me give you an example, I once got a call to do an emergency run from a refrigeration company to deliver a much needed refrigeration part to a restaurant located near the Empire State building. Can you believe that the manufacturer was three states away from New York City? The urgency was that this restaurant had thousands of dollars' worth of frozen and fresh food that was about to spoil if the part was not delivered immediately. The part only cost $125.00 but the delivery cost was $225.00. To this restaurant the $350.00 was nothing compared to losing thousands of dollars in food.

Local, State and Federal governmental agencies ~ Government agencies will subcontract courier services to local businesses. This type of work can range from a simple document delivery to the use of tractor trailers. You will need to dedicate a great deal of energy into researching what jobs are available for contracting but there is great reward for your energy. This is how the process works. The government sends out bid request to individuals and businesses who are interested in doing the work. You will receive a complete outline of what their expectations are and any special requirements you need to have in order to be awarded the work.

There are several courier companies they prefer to award the bid too, like, female and minority business owners. If you do not fall into one of these categorize still offer your services because government agencies cannot discriminate just because you do not fall into one of these categories. Once you are awarded the contract you keep the work until the contracted work is done.

For example, there may be an environmental project that needs to have samples, which are gathered in the field, then delivered to the nearest Federal Department of Environment agency's office. This project is expected to last approximately twelve months. You will be the company who will do the work until the twelve months are completed.

How do you find out what jobs are being sent out for contract bidding? There are three methods for getting this information. 1) Government agencies website 2) A monthly publication sent out by the federal government 3) Independent businesses that specialize in assisting small business in getting government contracts. This whole process can be time consuming. I suggest you look into doing this type of work only after you have a solid customer base and can dedicate the needed time and energy into understanding the process. Local, State and Federal Government contracting is a great source of getting work even through it has its challenges in acquiring the work. But it's worth the time consumption and energy.

Medical and environmental laboratories ~ there are thousands of laboratories around our nation that use courier service. Medical laboratories will use courier companies to go to doctor offices, hospitals and clients to pick up blood work, urine and stool samples. You have perhaps noticed small boxes outside the doors of your doctor's office or dentist's office. These are used to place items that need to be picked up by a courier to then deliver to the nearest laboratory.

Environmental companies need the same type of courier service. I once did a job for an environmental company who was contracted to analyze the air quality of a school while asbestos was being removed. Three times a day for four months I drove to a school and received a packet that contained air to be delivered to the lab for analyzing. There is water samples, soil samples and even air samples that need to be taken from job sites to the lab.

Check clearinghouses ~ there are companies who contract with banks and check cashing agencies to process their checks in preparation for the Federal Reserve. There have been numerous changes in the rules and regulations of the Federal Reserve regarding the process of check cashing and transference of funds between banks. These changes have allowed the Federal Reserve to make bank to bank transfers electronically without the need for paper documentation. However, these check clearinghouses still need courier service. Not all of their customers are willing to transmit their checks electronically directly to the Federal Reserve because it's not always cost effective. Your ability to get courier work from these clearinghouses total depends on your tenacity. I encourage you to find one of these companies near you and add them into your sales cycle.

Finding them may not be easy as finding many of the other business and companies listed here in this book. You need to be crafty in locating them. I offer three suggestions: Do a web search – key words to use are 'check clearinghouses', 'check processors', or 'Federal Reserve check preparation'. The second suggestion is to speak to a bank officer to see if they know who and where these companies are located in your area. Of course you will need to establish a relationship with a bank officer but you should be doing that anyway. The third suggestion is to do research at your local library and at your local small business administration office. Once you find who they are and where they are located, swing by and see how you can best approach them in order to acquire work. Because of security regulations you need to approach these companies with wisdom. But don't allow this to intimate you…they need courier service and once you are in the door you will be able to present you and your service with good results.

Retail check cashing businesses ~ owners of retail check cashing business often have several locations. Sometime during the course of the business day all the checks from these various locations need to be gathered and delivered to the central office or to a check cashing clearinghouse. These retail operations are easily located and are always willing to discuss how they can improve their service or save pick-up and delivery cost.

As you see there are numerous businesses and companies who use and need courier service. As you venture out you will see that what I have provided you is only scratching the surface. I have giving you enough information to start and grow your business in any direction you desire. Always be on the lookout for how you can grow your business by caring for the needs of your customers. Now that you have suggested businesses to approach lets discuss how to approach them in order for them to give you their business. The next few chapters discuss how & where to find them, your most valuable business tool and sales and marketing.

Chapter 7

Where & How to Find Customers

Now that you know what type of companies and businesses use courier service lets discuss how you can locate those new customers by keeping in mind how you are going to incorporate these contacts into your marketing plan.

Start with who you know – family, friends and associates. Let the word of your new business to get into the ears of those who have an interest in helping you get started. Make sure you have your business cards ready for those individuals so they can begin to hand them out for you.

Yellow pages – Looking for companies and businesses in the yellow pages is helpful. Not a lot of information is given in the phone book but it gives you a general idea where you can start to locate them.

Web searches – get on line and do searches for businesses in your area. Bing, Yahoo, Google, etc… are more valuable sources of information. You can find addresses, maps, phone numbers, and even contact information.

Library – go to your local library and you will find reference material listings of local business and companies. I will often spend a few hours a month researching new potential companies using this method. By the way, libraries also use courier services. When a library has several locations patrons have the ability to drop off books, music CD and movies. There items need to get back to their original location. Offer your services.

Drive bys – drive around and look for companies. I have found this profitable. There are 'hole in wall' places where businesses will hide. Find an industrial or a business park and you will find a goldmine of potential new businesses and companies for you to approach.

Other courier services – in another chapter there is a discussion about how to form a relationship with other courier companies. If a courier company has been established for years they, more than likely, have settled into the type of work they do and will turn down new businesses. (Don't let this happen to you) and will let other courier companies in on the business they cannot handle. If you approach them correctly and build a working relationship with them, they can be a source of new business for you.

Look n listen – all around you are newspapers, bill board advertisements, radio ads etc… train your eyes and ears to look for that next potential customer.

Sales lead services- there are business to whom you can pay to gather leads for you. Don't start your business this way. Why pay someone when you can do the research for yourself? However, if you think that using a sales lead service will get you attractive business by all means use one.

Bidding services – there are companies that bid for various work then outsource the work. Often they will bid on national work then contract out the work to local companies. You can find these bidding companies by doing web searches. Contact them and let them know where you are located and to contact you if there are any contracts they are bidding on in your area. Be open and honest with your ability. They are looking for individuals and businesses they can trust with outsourcing. R. R. Donnelly is a national bidding contract company who bids on local and regional courier routes. Call them and see if there is any work in your area that they can contract out to your courier service.

Chapter 8

Your best business tool – the business card

Business cards are a must! Even in this high tech world the business card is your most valuable tool. It is the first piece of information, other than yourself, which communicates to your customer and potential customer. Business cards are simple, inexpensive and effective. In order to maximize the business card's effectiveness there are a few rules that must be followed.

~ **Keep the card simple!** Do not over burden your card with too much information and design. All you need is the name of the company, your name and contact information. Contact information should include your cell phone number and if you have a website, include the address. You can include other information such as distinguishing characteristics of your company that sets you apart from your competitors. If your Tag-line is not to long then add it to your business card. But that is all you need. The goal is to provide information that communicates how your customer is best able to contact you. If they need any additional information then they can call you and ask you for what they need.

~ **Always carry your cards with you!** Even on your 'days off'. Keep a supply in your car, in your wallet or any place else that makes the cards within an arm's reach. Do you work out at the gym? Take cards with you. Do you go to church? Take the cards with you. Do you attend functions and events? Take the cards with you. You will find that even the most casual conversation may turn into a business opportunity.

~**When you hand out your card maintain a positive, confident, can do attitude!** It is during this time that you will be asked about your service. Questions like 'do you go to so and so?' Can you handle several boxes?' or 'Can you pick up at this particular hour and have it delivered by the end of the day?' Whatever the question, you must have a confident, positive, can do attitude to make the customer or potential customer feel at ease with you and your ability. If you have a look of perplexity or doubt the customer will not feel comfortable with handing you important documents or items. Does this mean you lie? Never! Trust is important and once trust is lost it may never be regained.

~**Learn how to overcome obstacles!** Your goal is to leave a card. Sometimes individuals don't want to receive your card, so you must hear the reason with a gracious smile but somehow insist they take your card. Allow me to share two short stories.

Once, I visited a mortgage company and the receptionist insisted they have no need for courier service. I simply left my card on her desk, smiled and said 'you never know what might happen next' then I walked away. Can you believe that before the week was over she called me to rush an application to a title company? The job was an hour long and I made $45.00 and best of all, they call me whenever they need something delivered.

Another time I approached a Data Processing company and I was told there was no need to leave a card because they have their own drivers. I ignored the no and left my card anyway. After a week I was called because one of their drivers had to take some emergency time off. I covered his work for two weeks and during that time the companies' client base grew so that when their driver returned I received the extra work load. These stories, and there are more, simply illustrate that when you have the opportunity to leave a card – Leave the card! It may turn into a money making opportunity.

Another trick I have used with success is to ask for their card first. There are 'business card rules' which suggest that you are to wait until someone offers their card first before you ask. I disagree. Your goal is to acquire new business and business cards are the best way of communicating you and your service. My view is they want you to have their card. So when they hand you their card it is business etiquette for them to accept your card.

Do not waste their contact information.

When you receive a business card treat that card like a million $ bill, because that is exactly what its potential is to you and your business.

Here are a few simple instructions:

1. Protect the card by placing it in a safe place. Keeping all the business cards you have received in a location that is quickly and easily assessable. My suggestion is in a briefcase that is kept in your car.

2. Transfer the card information into an electronic contact software program. This duplication will be useful when you send out emails and make phone calls.

3. Follow up with an email or phone call. As with all business contacts, follow up is important. Even the simple exchange of business cards should be followed up with some sort of follow up.

4. Do not toss away any cards, even years later. You never know when you will need that contact information. Once I was asked in a causal business meeting about an individual I had had contact with years earlier. I was asked if I knew how to contact him in order to assist in a business transaction. I simply walked to my car and retrieved the business card. This so impressed the business owner I was given more work.

5. Weekly flip through cards to assist you in keeping a mental notebook of who's who and what's what. This will keep you sharp by reminding you who you spoke with, what their business is like and how you can provide your service.

Chapter 9

How to Get Customers – Sales and Marketing 101

Marketing and Sales - marketing and sales are not the same thing. They work together to get business for your business. Marketing is the activities and strategies which produce results in making products and services available that satisfy customers while making profits for the companies that offer those products and services. While sales is the process or steps to move a product or a service into the hands of a paying customer. How does this apply to your business? Basically, what are you going to do to get business?

Marketing & sales can become complex and philosophical but don't fall into that trap. This manual has a simple and easy marketing and selling plan for you to follow to produce the results you desire. By following the outlined activities you will avoid disappointment and discouragement. Does it mean you don't have to work at it…God forbid that attitude. If you work the plan the plan will work for you.

Developing a Marketing Plan – Don't make marketing complex. There is no need to reinvent the marketing wheel. You can develop your own but you will find that the plan in this book is proven, simple, easy to implement, fun, adventurous and profitable. This plan will keep you busy for years to come if you live around a large city town or small town. Once you start you will begin to see fruit in approaching your business according to this marketing plan and sales strategies.

There are two marketing plans that will get you started with confidence. Start with either one because both plans are productive. But before we discuss the two plans you need a Marketing and Sales notebook.

Marketing & Sales Notebook - This notebook is where you will keep track of all your marketing and sales. Use a two inch three ring binder with alphabetical page dividers which you will keep track of all your perspective customers.

- Give each potential customer their own page and file their page using the alphabetical page dividers.

- On each page record potential customers information, such as, company name, address, phone numbers including main number and fax number, website, email address, the name of the first person you spoke too, name of gatekeeper, and name of the individual who manages the dispatching of courier items. If the potential customer has other locations record each of those locations with their same information.

- Record the date & time of each visit and phone call you make in the margin of the page. Record how the conversation went as well as any progress in your business relationship with that company.

- Over time these potential customers will become customers (some more quickly than others...I had one customer that took seven years to acquire. It ended up being a multimillion dollar contract with a healthy profit line but more about that later in this chapter), so it's important to record all relevant information.

- Review your Sales and Marketing notebook from beginning to end at least once a week. This will trigger you into action, whether that action is a phone call, getting a quote to them, sending them information about your company, sending them a sales follow-up letter, etc.

- As your notebook gets filled with potential customers you will naturally see a pattern to your sales and marketing method. Use this feedback to make adjustment to your plan and to your sales strategies.

- Keep this notebook close to your chest. That means don't share it with anyone. If you ever come to the point where you desire to sell your company you can include this notebook as a selling feature. If you hire a sale person then you can share the information but don't simply give it to them to use. Encourage them to start their own, make a copy of their contacts and you place that contact into your notebook.

Two Marketing Plans

Now that you have your notebook ready here are the two plans you are to follow.

1. Market a particular business group – for example. If you would like to do work for banks then get a complete list of banks in your area. ALL OF THEM! Then systematically begin to visit each bank and keep track of all the information you gather by placing it into your marketing notebook. After exhausting all the banks in your area start marketing to another business group. Continue to market each group one right after the other. As you are doing courier runs and getting comfortable with your routine do not neglect your marketing plan it is your key to growth.

The advantage to this style of marketing is that you will begin to understand the type of work and what expectations this particular group needs to have accomplished. As your understanding increases you will begin to hear the same sales objections over and over again. This is good for you to experience because you will become a master in handling objections that are common within a business group.

Another advantage is that once you acquire your first customer in this group you will find that others will trust you and your work if you already are doing work for another company in the same business. It is perfectly acceptable to mention in your opening sales pitch that you do work for 'such & such' company. You may receive a blank stare but the wheels are turning in the mind of your potential customer, that if you are already doing this type of work then they should consider offering you work.

2. Market a particular location – towns and cities generally have business districts with their jurisdiction. Find out where these business centers are and start introducing yourself & your service. After you completed your initial contact make sure you place the information of the company you visited in your marking notebook.

This type of marketing will expose you to all sorts of companies and businesses which will you should use to your sales advantage. There will be diversity in the sales objections you will hear and you might get tripped up when addressing them but after you visit a number of businesses you will settle in and get comfortable in dealing with diversity.

This is a good marketing plan when you already have a customer in that general area. Let's say you have a pick-up in the area. Arrive a few minutes early and begin to walk into business and introduce yourself and your service and let them know that you do work for 'such & such' company and since you were in the area you thought you could stop by and see if their company could use your service.

Implementing a marketing plan into action means you are going to go get sales. Remember, your aim is to attract and keep a steady group of loyal and paying customers. As well as expanding your customer base by identifying and attracting new customers by anticipating market shifts and risk assessment that can affect your bottom line. This may seem confusing at first but as you expand your personal & business development all of this will make sense to you.

Now that you have a marketing plan how do sales fit into that plan?

Sales – There are many books and seminars that focus on the success of selling and by all means spend time learning how to sell and improving your sales skills. The art of selling is a life time learning experience. Even the most successful sales people are always learning. But start here with the information provided to get your business up and running. This will get your feet wet and in the doors of potential customers. Please get away from thinking that if you place an ad in the local paper or set up a website that you will be overloaded with customers. If you want your business to grow then you must get out there and go get the customer. Place your marketing and sales plan into action…don't wait for the customer to come to you. There will be a time when individuals, businesses and companies will be approaching you to do work for them but don't count on that for at least a year or two. You must go get customers.

There is a selling cycle that you will be consistently involved in with all your potential customers. Keep track of this cycle with the help of your Marketing & Sales notebook. Rewrite this cycle in your own words on a single piece of paper and place it into the front of your notebook. This will be a handy quick reference for you to keep your sales activities in a healthy perspective.

The Selling Cycle – becoming familiar with the cycle will be a valuable aid in guiding you to success. Some parts of this cycle will be natural and other parts will need to be developed. Study this cycle until it becomes part of your natural mental process in your day to day activities.

~ **Prospecting** – means finding the right business that will benefit from your service. Chapter 6 is a list of types businesses and companies that use courier service. Now you need to find those types of customers that are in your area.

~ **Contact** – once you find a company to approach it's time to establishing contact. The initial contact with the company will more than likely be with a receptionist or a secretary. These individuals can provide you with valuable information that you will enter into your notebook. Get as much information as you can from these individuals. Once you have established contact and made a short presentation you need to ask questions. Do this with politeness and clarity. Your goal is to qualify the business, can this particular company benefit from your service and do you want to do work for this company?

~ **Qualification** – the potential customer will be qualifying you and you will be qualifying the customer. The potential customer will be thinking… Do I like this individual? Can I trust this individual? Can you provide the service you are saying you can provide? After your presentation the potential customer will begin to ask you questions. At the same time you need to be qualifying the potential customer.

~ **Presentation** – Now that you have established contact and have gone through the qualification phase it's time to make a solid presentation to the decision maker. Your presentation may take a few minutes or 30 minutes. The goal here is to ensure that the potential customer has a good understanding of who you are and what services you can provide. During the presentation the decision maker is taking the qualification step to a deeper level and they will become verbal with their thoughts and begin to ask you questions. You will learn a lot from the types of questions they ask you. Take mental notes – are they concern about timing of delivery? Are they concerned about insurance? Are they concern about confidentiality? Are they concerned about invoicing and billing? Answer their questions with clarity and honesty.

Special Note: *Always ask the potential customer what is their biggest challenge in their business with regards to courier service. This is a great question because it cuts through to the heart of their concerns. It maybe pricing, timeliness, it may be problems the courier service they are now using. Listen with intent because whatever the challenge is with their current courier service you are going to be the solution. Let them know that you understand the challenge and that you can and will provide outstanding service. Lay out your plan in solving their challenge. This approach has always open door of business to me.*

~ **Objections** – the next thing you will encounter is objections. The potential customer will begin to think of reasons why they don't need your service. You will hear things like… 'We have our own drivers?' 'We have an established relationship with another courier service'. You might hear 'I will think it over?' How are you to hand these and other types of objections?

Special Note: *Whenever you hear objections write them down in a special section of your Marketing & Sales Notebook and over the course of time you will hear all the possible objections. While you are writing them in your notebook think of how you should handle the objections. Review them from time to time so that you will, in a natural manner, be able to address the objections with success.*

Steps in overcoming objections:

Step #1 Listen… don't be quick to address the objection before the customer has the chance to finish saying what is on their mind. If at all possible get all their objections before you begin to answer the first objection. Simply say…'I understand your concern is there anything else that is a concern to you?' Once the objections are spoken prepare your response by addressing the important ones first.

Step #2 Repeat the objection… restating the objection back to the customer using their own words is a way of getting them to understand that you identify with the objection. If you do not understand the concern then ask the customer to clarify. Make sure you and the customer are on the same page.

Step #3 Answer it… when you have the whole story about their objection then answer the objection. Start your answer with an assurance. Use words like 'I know how you feel…' 'I understand your concern…' 'I know what you're saying because…' Objections are either based on facts or on emotions. Dealing with factual objections is easy but the emotional objections can be more challenging. Answer the objection with clarity and honesty. If you have dealt with the objection with a different customer relay how you address that concern… give examples. Use stories of past experiences. Simply tell them how you can handle their concern.

Step #4 Confirm your answer…ask them if what you just said address their concern. This gives them the chance to understand you and how you are going to address their concern. At this point the conversation will go into one of three directions…another objection, a delay in making a decision or the closing of the sale.

Step #5 Move on… once you have dealt with the objections move the conversation to another topic. Here is where you want to guide your potential customer away from the objections and onto another topic. Just make sure the next topic of discussion is relevant or your potential customer will think that you can't handle their objections. The next topic should guide your potential into closing the sale but don't jump into the close without making a smooth transition. Be sensitive and make sure your timing is on target.

~ Closing the sale – Ask the potential this question, 'When can we start?' at this point the potential will lay out the start date or lay out conditions that need to be satisfy before you can start the work. Conditions are no big deal they are just business details that need to be dealt with. Such as pricing, insurance documentations, informing key people of the decision before you can start the work. Whatever these conditions are make sure they are dealt with quickly.

~ Benign Encroachment – I love benign encroachment! It has served me well in acquiring new business. But what in the world is benign encroachment? It is how you approach a customer to acquire more of their courier business. Once you have come to terms and you are doing the work for your new customer and MAKING SURE you are doing a GREAT job in the service you provide…you can begin to approach your new customer in a benign manner as you encroach into their business with the goal to be the only courier company they use. Often when you start doing work for a new customer they will have some strings attached to their old courier service. Don't be surprised if that old courier service is still around and doing work. Your goal is to get them out of the door.

How do you do this? First of all, do not criticize the other courier company. Even if they are doing a poor job, keep your mouth shut because if you can see that they are doing a poor job so does your new customer. Secondly, always remain happy, positive and willing to do whatever it takes to satisfy your new customer. By this time you have established a good and health working relationship with those who you interact with each time you do a courier run. Thirdly, look for opportunity. Is there an emergency run that needs to be delivered? Do it like it's no problem. Is there a new run being developed? Offer your services by saying 'I can do that'. Did someone in the organization mess up and you can bail them out? Bail them out without making a big 'to do' about it. Once, I had a bank customer accidentally delivered $30,000 cash to the wrong check cashing company. I was pulled into a back office and asked if I could help without billing the company. Absolute! That single act allowed me to acquire more business from that individual, because I was willing to go the extra mile and help without making it obvious. Be smooth and helpful in any challenge your new customer has and you will see that benign encroachment will help you grow your business.

~ **Leads** – now that you have a new customer and you have placed that customer into your daily schedule of activities, it's time to look for that next lead that the new customer can provide. After a few weeks of satisfying your new customer, approach them to see if they know of any other business that could benefit from you service. This is a great way to get new customers. Businesses develop a network of individuals and other companies over the years and this networking can increase your business simply by approaching your new customer and asking them if they know of anyone who could use your service.

How long you are in the sales cycle with a potential customer depends on your diligence and the customer's trust and timing. Not everything is in your control but you need to stay on top of the things you have control over. Your goal is to keep the sales cycle as short as possible. There will be times when you will go through this cycle in a few minutes and began to do work almost immediately. But if you see that the customer is not interested in you or your service come up with a way to keep the contact and the relationship open to future possibilities. As the saying goes 'keep the ball in play'.

Developing a sales attitude – perhaps the single most effective tool in sales is having the proper sales attitude. This attitude is not hard to develop and maintain. Allow the right attitude to work into your personal style. Make adjustments to your personality and presentation will give you the business fruit you are looking for…profit!

~ Be yourself – don't force yourself into some super sales man, thinking that if you become someone you're not that you will be successful at sales. Admittedly, salesmanship comes easy for some and difficult for others. If sales are difficult for you, learn how to work thru your fears, shyness, nervousness, or whatever else is standing in your way of going out and doing what needs to be done. It's important that you develop a lifestyle of presenting yourself and if you try to become someone you're not you are damaging yourself and the growth of your business. Fakeness is transparent and if your potential customer can see right through the fakeness and decide to give their business to someone they can trust. Relax…be yourself.

~ Be positive – a positive spirit goes a long way in this negative world. Start your day off right and get rid of those negative impressions that burden the hearts and souls of men and women. Greet everyone you encounter with a smile and a kind word because it opens doors of opportunity. Review the section of mastering negative thinking in the self-management section to get the upper hand on developing a positive disposition.

~ Be confident – confidence comes with getting your act together. This book, if properly followed, is foundational to developing a confidence that will lead you to success. Gaining experience is next in developing a confident attitude and there is no best way to get experience then to go out and start selling yourself and your service. If you have never been involved in the sales process before, you will make mistakes….so what! We all make mistakes. Learning from those mistakes is the best way to get the experience. Conveying a confident spirit is easier when you are confident and knowing who you are and what you can do.

~ Be tenacious – Don't give up! Failure and rejection will have its effect on you so learn from them and learn how to deal with those situations that causes you to want to toss in the towel and give up. Tenaciousness in sales is perhaps the number one attitude you need to maintain when everything seems to be going wrong in an individual sale or in the sales cycle. When you have those feelings of giving up, step back relax, regain your energy and jump back into the sales mode. The more potential customers you place in the sales cycle the more productive your efforts will bear you profitable fruit. Being tenacious not only with adding more potential customers into the sales cycle but be tenacious in dealing with those potential customers who seem more challenging to satisfy.

~ Be patient – being patient with yourself and with the sales cycle is not easy. We live in a culture that says 'I got to have it now'. As the saying goes 'Rome was not built in a day'. When you feel the pressure of impatience creep up on you during the sales cycle you will begin to force something that may cost you more then you bargain for. Relax, trust yourself and trust the sales cycle. Keep things in perspective. Things won't always happen when you want them to nor will things go as you plan and hope for…that's okay. Be patient and keep working.

~ Be clean - please forgive me for having to deal with this topic but I must because I have seen couriers who in my opinion were dirty and disgusting. Personal hygiene needs some attention. To my amazement there are couriers who wear sweat pants, ripped tee shirts and oily baseball hats. That's fine on a Saturday morning lounge around the house but it's not right to look that way in a business environment. I cannot understand how individuals think they can walk into a place of business with that sort of attire. I strongly encourage you to look and be a respectable business owner and manager.

Here are my suggestions:

1. Take care of your body… if you are out of shape, get into shape. Lose weight, stop smoking, hit the gym, or get running, biking or whatever you enjoy to get you back into top physical shape. Why? Because you will feel better and look better to you and your customers! Sitting in a car for hours upon hours a day can turn your body and mind into mush.

2. Shower and shave daily. If you have facial hair, keep it neat and trim.

3. Comb your hair, brush your teeth, wash your hands, use deodorant or anti-perspiration and trim your nails.

4. Wear attractive, business casual clothing and make sure they are clean. Don't wear shorts, sneakers and a tee shirt. Look professional by wearing nice and neat pants. I have learned that jeans are okay but make sure they are clean and fit you properly. Polo shirts are good but why not wear dress shirts. You don't have to get fancy but there are a lot of nice dress shirts that are relaxing and professional in appearance.

Sales and marketing is how you are going to get your business up and running. It is also how you are going to grow your business and it's how you are going to stay in business. No matter how busy you are with all the other aspects of maintaining your business do not neglect sales and marketing. After you place a new customer into you daily courier routine, begin to look for that next customer.

Chapter 10

Insuring success – Self Management

The number one reason for business failure is not lack of funding or poor location or competition or lack of business skill and knowledge or any other reason you may have heard as an excuse. The number one reason for business failure is poor self-management. Think about it… if an individual can properly manage themselves, all sorts of challenges that causes failure will fall by the way side and nothing will prevail except success.

What is self-management? It is how an individual manages their thoughts, attitudes, values, and actions. As you can see self-management affects all the various aspects of our lives. It affects all of our relationships, our time, our resources, our work, and just about all of our situations.

The focus of this section is to narrow self-management in the area of how to improve our self-management skills to succeed in starting, owning and managing a courier service. Read this section often and expand your reading on this topic from other individuals to build a solid foundation that will guide you through failures and challenges.

Self-management skills are also called adaptive skill. How are you going to adapt to your new desire to start your own company? What are the new rules and principles that need to be developed to insure success? What's in your work ethic that needs to be changed to maximize your energy and time? What is your personal work style? How are you going to be influenced and how are you going to influence others? What will be the attitude you have to your new work and work environment? It's clear that this book will not be able to answer all these questions for you and your personal situation but this topic needs to be discuss in order to get you started and on the road to personal and business success.

Positive self-awareness – the world around us can be rather negative, just turn on the 6 o'clock news and you will see and hear the negative that's lurking in the world. Then there are 'those people' who no matter how good and positive a situation can be will toss a wet towel on the positive and suck the life out of us. So let's be honest, if we are going to change the negative into positive we must start with ourselves. We must develop a healthy self-awareness and that starts with our thoughts. These thoughts convert into action and our actions determine the level of our success.

Managing your thoughts – self-defeating thoughts can kill a person. They can lead down a path of failure and self-destruction. The mental and verbal 'put-downs' can be difficult for some people to deal with. There are many factors that contribute to negative thinking. Family background, how we were raised, past failures in intimate relationships, negative comments from family members and past efforts that did not succeed into the dreams we had. But whatever the causes for these negative thoughts victory must and will be achieve. Everyone at some point in their life has to deal with negative thoughts especially during the time of altering the direction of our lives. So how do we deal with negative thoughts?

Self-defeating thoughts sound like a never ending tape recording that repeats over and over in our mind. Even when we think we have victory over them they never give up and have a way of sneaking back into our minds when we least expect them too.

Thoughts like:
- I'm not good at anything.
- Everything I do end up in failure
- What's the use in starting up my own business because I don't have what it takes?
- It's too late in my life to make this kind of change in my career.
- I'm such an idiot…why did I do that?

Often these negative thoughts can be attached to a person, a situation or a past failure. We need to put those people, those situations, and those failures behind us and learn to turn these negative thoughts into positive thoughts.

- It can't be done ...change it into...I can do it!
- I hate change.........................change is normal!
- It's impossible........................I'm possible!
- I make a terrible mistake............I made the best decision at the time!
- I don't have much hope.............I expect to succeed!

Take the extra time to write down the negative thoughts that you have heard over the years and spin them into positive thoughts. This is a good practice to do because you need to master over those negatives each time they enter into your head and heart. Write them down and spin them around. Consider extra reading material or attend a seminar or discuss this issue with a friend or see a pastor or counselor....bottom line is for you do what it takes to master these negative thoughts and declare victory in order to succeed in your new business venture.

Fighting excuses – There are Hebrew proverbs found in the Bible that point to men who find excuses so over powering that there is nothing but poverty and destruction as a spoiled fruit. But the promise of overcoming excuses and being diligent will produce joy, satisfaction and rewards.

"The sluggard says, 'There is a lion in the road! A lion is in the open square!'"
Proverbs 26:13

"The sluggard says, "There is a lion outside; I will be killed in the street!'
Proverbs 22:13

"A lazy man does not roast his prey, but the precious possession of a man is diligence."   Proverbs 12:27

"Poor is he who works with negligent hand, But the hand of the diligent makes rich."   Proverbs 10: 4

"The plans of the diligent lead surely to advantage…"
Proverbs 21:5

"The soul of the sluggard craves and gets nothing, but the soul of the diligent is made fat." Proverbs 13:4

59

At the heart of excuses and lack of productivity is laziness. For some there is no hope but for others who face laziness there can be a great reward and pleasant surprises. Examine your heart each time you feel like giving into an excuse for not getting your business done. Write them down then consider what the outcome will be if you give into the excuses for laziness. Then do the same thing you do with negative thoughts. Spin them around into reasons for getting the work done. Start off with small easily attainable rewards. For example, perhaps there is that moment you don't want to work but instead stay in bed or sit on the couch and watch TV or watch a worthless movie. Make an agreement with yourself that if you work for the next few hours and get a particular task accomplished you will reward yourself. Keep your reward small but effective in getting you moving. For example, rewards yourself with a walk around the block or a game of racket ball or favorite snack of ice cream. This may seem like a Jedi mind trick that you're playing on yourself but practice doing it and you will gain the upper hand in overcoming laziness and giving into excuses.

Do an assets and liabilities inventory – take stock of yourself and determine what positive personal qualities and traits you have. Write them down and even review them with a family member or friend because they can give you even more positive qualities. Also, support what you have considered as an asset with an example. Are you honest? Then think of an example of when you were honest. Are you reliable? Then think of an example of when you were reliable. Even have your family member or friend help you think of examples that demonstrate the asset. Use your imagination in exploring positive traits.

Here are some positive traits (assets) to get you started:

Adaptive	Curious	Informed	Reasonable
Ambitious	Decisive	Intelligent	Reliable
Analytical	Dedicated	Loyal	Resourceful
Artistic	Disciplined	Mature	Responsible
Assertive	Educated	Moral	Self-assured
Capable	Energetic	Neat	Smart
Careful	Enthusiastic	Optimistic	Spontaneous
Competent	Ethical	Organized	Stable
Competitive	Fair	Perceptive	Strong
Confident	Flexible	Persistent	Sympathetic
Conscientious	Forceful	Polite	Tactful
Considerate	Friendly	Positive	Thorough
Cooperative	Handy	Practical	Thoughtful
Courageous	Helpful	Precise	Tolerant
Creative	Honest	Progressive	Trusting
Courteous	Idealistic	Quick	Unselfish

Always be careful when doing this type of exercise because strength can turn into a weakness but the flip side is that a weakness can become strength. No matter what you consider your traits to be they need improvement and they will be put to the test as you start your new business. The same goes for your weaknesses. Starting, owning and managing your own business will expose your weaknesses. Consider this to be positive because when they are exposed you can improve them. The goal here is to take an inventory so you know what areas in your life need self-management to insure success.

As you begin to add staff to your business this asset & liability inventory will naturally be applied to those whom you are considering hiring. By placing yourself under this process you will gain the knowledge and skills to build yourself a successful team to meet the needs of your customers and increase business success and profitability.

Now it's time for you to fly! – As a young boy I remember growing up on the family farm spending countless hours walking the fields and riding tractors. I would often look up and see airplanes flying by. And as the mind of little boys travel I wondered how in the world do those things stay in the air? Of course as the years went by I came to understand how they stayed in the air. Yeah, there are principles of flight and a bunch of mechanics that works with those principles to keep that plane in the air. But simply put, it's an engine with two wings. And that how you need to view an aspect of self-management.

An airplane flies with two wings and an engine and the same applies to starting and managing your new business venture. The engine is your business and it needs to be fueled to provide your wanted result… success. And success in this case is profitability. As we have discussed in another chapter that cash flow is the fuel to getting your business up in the air. And once your business is up in the air there are two things that you need to stabilize the flight. And they are discipline and desire. Discipline and desire directly applies to self-management. Let's discuss desire first.

Desire is that which motivates you to do the things you like and love to do that generates a profitable business. All of us enjoy doing certain aspects of our business simply because we find them easy and gain a certain amount of pleasure and satisfaction from them. What we each desire to do is different from individual to individual. Some enjoy sales more than others, some enjoy phone calls more than others while others prefer to shut the office door and do book keeping and computer work. And of course there are varying amounts of degrees in the things we do that generate varying amounts of pleasure and satisfaction. This all seems like common sense however this all needs to be understood because you need to self-manage your desires. If you focus too much attention on the things that you find easy to do because you like to do them then you potentially will lose focus on doing those things that need to be accomplished in order for your business to stay in the air. That's where the wing of discipline balances out your flight and successfully allows you to reach your destination.

You need to manage those things that are challenging, hard, uncomfortable, time consuming and things you simply don't like to do. There are those phone calls that need to be made but you don't want to pick up the phone. There is that new business that opened a new office and you know they need courier service between the two offices but you don't feel like stopping by and handing out your business card. There are insurance issues you really need to handle but you don't like dealing with the insurance agency. There are those invoices that need to be calculated but you don't like sitting and working on them. And there are those days that you simply don't feel like getting in your car today….whatever it is that you don't want to do but needs to be done requires discipline.

There are skills that assist in being disciplined and those skills need to be explored and mastered in order to achieve business success. Learn what makes you motivated is all part of self-management. We all have 'those days' that seem more challenging and difficult and the quicker you are in mastering yourself the quicker you will be successful in your business. Keep your business moving through desire and discipline. Now let's turn our attention on a specific area that will help you improve your self-management.

Isolation – Small business owner's isolation has been the cause of numerous small business failures. Don't allow this to become your fate. There are several options that have assisted business owners in overcoming isolation. This must become part of your self-management. Here are several suggestions for you in overcoming small business isolation but it's up to you to choose those options that will keep your chin up during those days when you feel like you're the only one out there facing this challenge.

~ Find an emotional partner – there is no need for you to start this business venture without emotional support. This is often over looked when it comes to the business world but you will find it extremely helpful. We will discuss business partnership in another chapter but in overcoming business isolation it is suggested that you find someone or several people with whom you can generate a safe and healthy relationship. Choose wisely! This is going to be an individual with whom you will share your joys and your sorrows. It should be someone who has a special care and love for you and your success, perhaps a parent, a sibling, a close friend or someone from your church. Exchange cell phone numbers because you will want to be able to contact this individual whenever you feel like things are to challenging or you are simply having a bad day. When you are feeling 'down' or are faced with giving up give this individual a call and don't hold back; express the situation and how you feel. Most of the time all you will need is a listening ear. You will see that as you communicate your thoughts that you can often build yourself back up. Sometimes all that is need is a few questions from your partner to refocus your attention off your challenging situation and on to the task you have at hand.

~ Get a mentor – there are hundreds of successful business men and women who have already traveled down the path you now find yourself traveling. Use their experience, wisdom and insight in assisting you in your new business endeavor. You can become as close to your mentor as you and they are willing but you will find that the closer you are to your mentor the richer the experience. You will have lots of unanswered questions that go beyond this book and it's great to have someone else around to whom you can go to for that extra advice. Once you have chosen your mentor hand them a copy of this book. This will give them an understanding of what you are going to accomplish and they can offer you deeper insight in business direction and decisions. Review this chapter with them and discuss what you believe are your strengths and weakness as reflected in is section of this manual and see if they can provide additional information to you.

Never ask your mentor for money. Always express your gratitude. When you follow their advice and it is profitable then let them know. Even if the advice you followed did not turn out as plan... tell them. You can be reassured that they can tweak their advice and sharpen it so you will not lose ground in business growth. Always be honest with your problems and issues. Allow them to ask you difficult questions and without defending yourself or actions share with them your concerns and you will find the experience richer and profitable. Try not to bother your mentor with the mundane. Use your time and their time wisely. Use them to help you with strategic issues and critical planning. Be positive with your mentor and if you find yourself being negative allow your mentor to change the direction of your heart and mind. Remember they are your mentors so allow them to speak into your life but keep in mind that all decisions are yours and in the end it is you who will reap the rewards or face the consequence of poor decisions.

~ Form a 'band of brothers' - gather around you a small group of people who can come along your side to help guide you, guide your ideas and guide your business. Use them as a sounding board or counsel board. They are not going to be your board of directors leading you and your business into areas you don't desire. Instead they are to assist you when laying out a business plan, or helping you overcome a road block in getting a new customer or giving you a fresh idea in applying a new business principle. You will find their guidance and advice extremely profitable. As your sounding board they can open doors for you that you could not open. They also will advise you about other doors you should consider closing.

Keep your board to three to five members. Meet once a month or once every three months. Choose individuals who have business experience. They don't have to be in the same business as yours because there are many basic challenges that affect all business and there is no reason for you to struggle and learn all by yourself. Consider being part of another member's 'band of brothers'. At first you will not have to pay your band of brothers but as your business grows consider paying for their lunch and as your business continues to grow offer them $50.00 for each meeting they are able to attend. There are some decisions that they can assist you with but keep in mind that they are there to advice and offer assistance, the final decision is all yours.

Just imagine that you are having a problem with a particular employee who is always late and you're not sure what to do about it. Bring it to your band of brothers and see what solutions they have to offer. Perhaps there is a daily nagging problem that you encounter and its stands in the way of productivity and profitability. Your 'band of brothers' can see solutions that you overlooked or did not see at all.

~ Join business associations – there are numerous business associations that are local, regional, national and international. There are many advantages in joining a business association but there are limitations as well. You must decide which association will work best for you and your business. Consider joining a local business association or a regional or national that has a local office or branch. A great place to start looking for business associations is your local library. A well-funded library has a good business resources section. Ask the librarian what resources they have for you and you will be surprised (at least I was) with the wealth of information the library generated. Another consideration in assisting you in researching an association is to do a web search. Include considering joining a courier industry associations. I personally have been disappointed with the courier industry associations because they did not provide me with fresh ideas, specific skills or any special knowledge that I was able use to generate more profitability.

Keep in mind that the goal in joining in an association is to prevent the illness of isolation from affecting you. So, when considering which associations to join, ask the question 'will it help me overcome small business isolation?' That is why it's perhaps more prudent for you to consider a local small business association rather than a regional or national organization. Also keep in mind that not everything you find in an association will be helpful. Don't get sucked into an association that will have nothing to offer you. If it will not help you, don't join. Some associations (especially national associations) will hit you up for money throughout the year….so consider carefully which, if any, you choose.

These associations have call centers and networking opportunities that you will find helpful. I know of a particular courier service that was having a difficult time acquiring addition insurance for a multimillion dollar financial institution account. The owner called the local association with whom he was a member and they were able to assist him in acquiring the needed additional insurance coverage.

~ Soak up information – the internet, magazines, books, CD, videos and audio tapes are useful in overcoming the feelings of small business isolation. Find that which works for you and your situation. I find it helpful that during a 'courier run down time' going into a bookstore and just looking at business book covers and reading excerpt from them cause me to feel refreshed in overcoming the feelings of isolation. You don't have to deal with starting and managing your own business all by yourself. Be creative and resourceful, use what is around you and form a team in providing you with success in business.

Conclusion: As you can see there is a great deal in self-management. What is provided for you here is by no means exclusive but it is a stepping stone for you to get your mind focused on those areas where you will need encouragement. The success of your business is entirely up to you. How bad do you want it? What changes are you willing to make to be successful? What are you will to sacrifice to gain profitability? No doubt you have what it takes to start and manage your own business. The road is wide open and you can take your business in any direction you desire but without proper self-management you will be doomed to failure and failure is not an option. So take the time, practice what is provided and do what needs to be done to get yourself under control.

Review this chapter and the chapter on time management often. Include additional material that will help you in specific areas of weakness. The goal is to know yourself and mastering yourself in order to provide you with a profitable and successful business.

Chapter 11

Time Management

Time management, like self-management, is important to any successful new business venture. Learning how to manage your time right from the start will make you and your business more productive. It's wise for you to develop a business culture that uses time wisely, first for yourself, then for your staff. As you learn how to master your time you will be able to master the time of others effectively. Time management is not hard nor challenging so learn the basic principles early.

There are loads of books, articles, CD, seminars and coaches that will load your head with cute little tricks to assist you in time management. This section will be addressing the specifics of time management and courier service. This chapter is divided into three sections: your personal time management, your customer's time management, your staff's time management. Come to terms quickly that if there is any business that needs to master time it's the courier industry. Your customers will depend on you to be the master of your time so they can trust you with their work. You can gain or lose customers if you wisely or unwisely use time.

Time management measurements - the management of time is difficult to measure and as the business owner it's up to you to determine if time is being wisely used. But how do you measure the effectiveness of time? The answer is results. But what do you use to measure results? The answer is planning and profitability.

Planning is important to any business. You need to plan out your year, months, weeks, days and hours. The best way to do this plan is to record (write it down) what you desire to accomplish within the year. Then break it down into quarterly sections (every three months), then into monthly sections, then into weekly sections then daily segments. Keep your yearly plan short and manageable by using a purpose, objectives and goals format. For example, what do you want to accomplish this year. That will be your purpose for the year. Then think about what objectives need to complete to arrive at your purpose. Goals are those bite size pieces of accomplishments that need to be completed in order to reach your objectives. The following is an example of a planning and format:

Purpose: Increase business by 100%

Objectives:
1) Acquire a new customer every four months.

Goals: - Contact a new business every week with a personal visit

- Revisit potential customers at least once a month with a phone call or a person visit

- Advertise in a local paper

2) Maintain a close connection with current customer base to do more work for them.

Goals: - Visit each company we do work for and inquire about doing additional work.

- Send out 'thank you' notes to each current customer

- Personally do one to two runs for them or join the independent subcontractor on a run.

3) Develop a relationship with another courier company to see if there is any work that you can do that will be beneficial and profitable to them and to your business.

Goals: - Research other local courier companies.

- Introduce myself and my company's service and delivery locations.

- Develop a trusting relationship with other company's owner or manager and call them or visit them monthly.

4) Research branching out into a different aspect of courier service.

Goals: - Review courier manual to see other branches of courier service.

- Research those companies via the web or yellow pages

- Make a list of potential new customers, add them to sales list and start marketing them.

Keep the purpose to a short, simple and achievable statement. As you think through the purpose your mind will begin to develop ways you can achieve the purpose. These are called objectives: what needs to be done to increase business 100%? Then, breaking down these objectives into bite size' actions which can be measured at any given time throughout the week and month. Apply this principal to all aspects of your business. Write it out and review it weekly to measure results and your time. This takes thought and time but you will find it helpful and profitable.

The other measurable result to see if time is being used wisely is profitability. Are you making money? How is the cash flow cycle? What is the company's monthly and weekly profit/loss statement telling about the company's financial health? Are you making the best time management decisions to produce a successful company? As your start your company you won't have much to measure how effectively you are using your time. Instead you will use other measurements to help determine how effective you are with your time. Over time you will see how productive you are with time management and using the principles in this manual will assist you.

Personal time management

No matter what phase of business growth you find yourself the idea of using your time wisely will bring about productivity and profitability. Once again what is presented here is not exclusive principles to time management so don't hesitate to research other people's ideas on the use of time.

~Get organized – taking the time to get organized is perhaps the most effective tool in mastering time management. The problem is that people don't take the time to get organized. Why? Because it takes time! But taking the time to get organized and taking the time to maintain organization will save you time, energy and frustration. For some individuals getting and staying organized is easy and fun but for others it will take a complete overhaul of their personality. Overhauling personalities is challenging however, the advantage is yours….start off your business right by starting off with the right habits. As your business grows and grows and it will, you will be doing yourself, your family, your customers and your staff a massive blessing by taking the time to organize yourself.

What needs to be organized?

First and foremost, your thoughts! In all the literature I've encountered about time management I have never come across anything that encourages people to organize their thoughts. This may sound ludicrous but give it a try and you will see the benefits of thought organization. It is especially helpful early in your work day when the fires and the rushes of the day are still under control. As your business begins to place more time pressure on you this process will allow you to work thru situations with more clarity and focus attention as well as prioritize your time.

This is what you do.

1. Get alone with several pieces of paper and a pen

2. Using short statements write down your thoughts about aspects of your work.

3. As you are processing what to write, other thoughts that don't pertain to work will begin to creep into your head. Write these down on a separate piece of paper.

4. Give yourself 10 to 15 minutes worth of time to record what is going thru your head.

5. At the end of your time, rewrite those thoughts into categorizes. Other things will enter your mind and that's okay. You will want to record them as well.

6. Categorizes might include things you want to do, things you need to do, problems that need to be solved, customers that need special attention. Some thoughts will be emotions reactions to an individual or a situation. Write it down. Write down things that are causing anxious and worrisome thoughts. Get it out of

your head and onto paper then review later when you have more time to consider a solution to the challenge. Whatever the thought place it in an understandable category.

7. Review these categories and prioritize what needs special attention.

8. Now place these thoughts where they need to be. For example, some thoughts need to be added to your 'to-do' list. Some thoughts need to be added to your appointment calendar. Some thoughts need to be written down so you can bring them up at your next staff meeting. You're basically turning your thoughts into actions.

9. Do this daily….at least during the first few months of your new business.

As time and business progresses you will want to do this at least at the beginning of each week. You will begin to see the fruit of thought organization within a few days. The more you practice this the more you will begin to be able to organize thoughts. The goal here is to train yourself to transfer thoughts into organized action.

There is another valuable tool which you will need to organize thoughts and that is… always and I mean ALWAYS have a pen and notepad with you. Have it near your bed at night. Have it when you walk out of the house. Have it with you as you go about your daily business routine. Have it with you when you talk to your staff. Have it with you when you drive in your car. Bottom line….always have it with you. Some people are blessed with superb memory, while the rest of us have to cheat and write down ideas, conversations, quotes, dates, times, contacts etc. Take the few seconds that it takes to write down important information and thoughts. Review this information daily and once again organize them into categories. This will guide you into prioritizing actions.

What else needs to be organized?

Your desk – work hard at keeping your desk neat and organized. It is impressive to see individuals who are able to maintain a clean, neat and organized desk. Here are a few tips:

~ At the end of each day make sure there is nothing on your desk. That way when you walk into your office your desk is ready to handle your day's activities.

~ Place useful and needed items in the same location each time. Put your pens into the pen holder. Store minimal items on your desk top. It's unsightly, troublesome and unprofessional to have a cluttered desk. Get into the right habit right from the start. This may seem trivial at first but as your business grows you will be thankful that you have developed an organized desk.

~ Use files for paperwork. This keeps your desk free of piles of papers such as schedules, invoices, bills, payroll etc. The most effective way is to use your desk drawers. And if there are not enough drawers consider getting a filing cabinet.

~ As a courier you will be traveling with a briefcase in your car. Have your briefcase near you when you work at your desk.

~ Keep your 'Master list' (you will learn what a master list is shortly) within eyesight but out of the way of the eyesight of others.

Your paperwork – it's amazing how businesses use so much paperwork and the courier industry is no different. Time sheet, travel sheets, log sheet, invoices, receipts, etc…and if you are not careful you will have piles and piles of papers surrounding you. Toss unimportant paperwork immediately and if there is doubt about how important it is, file it in temp folder until you are sure it can be tossed. Keep paperwork in categorizes and not in one giant heap. You will learn what categories you will need. Keep the paperwork off your desk and in files which are stored in your desk or filing cabinet. Try using small filing containers which are easily transported. If you find yourself with a growing pile of papers give it the attention it needs.

Your car – a detail discussion about what you will be traveling with in your car is in another chapter. So for the moment, focus on keeping your car clean and organized. Travel with your briefcase in the front passenger side seat. Keep mechanical tools in the trunk or in a place that is out of sight yet easily reached. If you travel with extra clothes (which is recommended) keep them in their own bag. Keep all insurance and registration paperwork in the glove box. Take out the day's trash at the end of each day, that means coffee cups, food wrappings etc.

Your briefcase – Only keep what you really need in your briefcase. If not it gets disorganized and heavy. What do you need in your briefcase? Pens, notepad, extra notepad, your marketing & sales notebook, a set of directions for each of your runs, business cards, cell phone, your daily planner and your Master list (to-do list).

Your conversations – using a phone log. This may seem strange to you but I picked up this trick from a British friend of mine and I have found it useful. Keep a spiral notebook with your cell phone. A regular size notebook will do just fine. Record each phone call that comes in or goes out. Note the date and time and any important information that comes from the conversation. Review this log at the end of the day and place any important information on your Master list or your 'to-do' list. There were times when I needed to review a conversation that I had with a customer about pricing, starting date for a new run and I would look into my phone log for what was said, who said what and when it was said. Very useful! Consider it a healthy back up.

Your computer –just like your office desk your computer has a desk top. Keep your computer uncluttered the same way you keep your desk uncluttered. Manage programs and files icons so that when you start up your computer you are not smacked in the face with a desk top that is disorganized. A simple way is to create files according to projects. For example, create a folder just for all your invoices (the discussion on invoicing is another chapter). That way when you need to research an invoice you know where to find it. When you need to create an invoice you know what folder to open up and start the new file. At first this will be easy but as business grows you will begin to get sloppy and place invoice where they don't belong and have a difficult time finding them in the future. Delete unwanted icons. Delete unused files. Delete unused programs. When you purchase a new computer if will be loaded with programs that you will not need – get rid of them.

The better organized you become the better time manager you will become. Taking the time to become better at organizing all aspects of your business life will increase your productivity and therefore your profitability. Start the practice of organization will turn into a healthy habit and you will be thankful that you did as you see how effective your life will be. Work at staying organized and you will see that you will be staying on top of specific project, develop new creative ideas; also putting out fires will be easier and dealing with staff and customers more effectively.

Tools of time management – every profession has tools. Mechanics have screwdrivers and sockets, doctors have stethoscopes and x-ray machines and surveyors have lasers and GPS systems. Tools allow individuals to become effective and efficient in accomplishing their jobs. As a business owner there are tools that will allow you to become effective and efficient in time management.

1) Daily planner – there are many styles of daily planners on the market. There are day planners, weekly planners, monthly planners and yearly planners. Get a planning system that allows you to record your year's activities (basically a calendar).

- Record pending meetings. Jot down who you're meeting with, the time and location of the meeting. Include what will be discussed at the meeting. For example, if you have meetings with a current customer to discuss the changes on a route place it in your daily planner and list these important items.

- Pending phone calls. Record all pending phone calls that you need to make. When your customer needs to follow up with you regarding a new account that they need to discuss with you and they ask you to call them back on such & such day, make sure you put it you're your calendar.

- Record birthdays, anniversaries of family, friends and important days for your customers. That way you can send them a gift, a card or make a phone call to celebrate that event in their life. It's important to review these events at the beginning of week that way you have plenty of time to buy a gift or card. This practice of sending out small gifts and cards has been overlooked by many business people. Use this to your advantage. This thoughtfulness will give you a better image in the mind of your customers. As a courier you will rub elbows with important employees of your customer, who can make your life easier to do your job. Include these individuals in your planning.

- Record your family and social activities. There is nothing more hurtful to a family member when a loved one has 'double' booked a business activity at the same time as a family event. This can be avoided by keeping track with your daily planner.

- Use a Daily planner system that functions with a computer program. Taking a few moments each day to transfer your daily planner information on to a computer program does a number of profitable things for you. First, it's a great back up encase you misplace or lose your daily planner. Secondly, the simple act of rewriting your information will help you keep better track of your time by reviewing important appointments. These programs use alarms and pop-ups to help you keep track of appointments. Just make sure you properly set the alarm.

Personal note: *I am partial to Microsoft products because of the ability to functionally integrations between programs. I have used the Microsoft calendar in their Office program as my daily planner. It has worked great for me. This has allowed me too easily, properly and functional keep track of my activities.*

2) A watch – This may sound simplistic but it's too important of a tool to overlook. That little item on the end of your wrist will keep you out of trouble. As you know I was raised on a family farm. When I was in my early teens there was a piece of land that we used to farm. We had road access to the field but we did not own the road access causing the field to be basically landlocked. This was not a problem because we had a great relationship with the land owner. Well, he passed away. He had no will or any known relatives and therefore the State was auctioning off his property. We were ready to bid on the property and we even had extra funds to ensure we won the bid. The date was set and on the day of the auctions my uncle and I got out of our farming clothes and slipped into our business clothes (a washed pair of jeans and a button down shirt). We looked at the clock hanging in the kitchen and determine when we needed to leave to attend the auction. We had plenty of time so we decided to take a walk in the fields to make proper use of our time. Well, what we neglected to do was take a watch with us and therefore missed the auction by a few minutes. Yikes….the new land owner knowing we needed the property sold the land to us for a profit of 100%. This was costly at the time but the lesson learned was good - keep track of time, and nothing works better than a watch.

Thankfully just about all cell phones have clocks and programmable alarms. And when your business is able to afford a smart phone service get one because of the great features that allow you to keep track of your time. Take the time and effort to learn how to program the alarms and sync your smart phone with your daily planners.

3) Master list – if there is any one thing that holds the most value to time management it's a Master list. The Master list or the 'to-do' list is the best tool to track your daily activities. By writing down everything that you need to get done will allow you to track and prioritize your work thus giving you more control over your activities and time.

- Use a legal size notepad as your Master list.

- Make sure you write on every line using legible writing.

- Number each item and use only one item per line.

- Use more than one page if needed.

- Don't just write down what you think you might get done that day but record all the things you need to get done, including large projects.

- Once your list is complete, start working on your tasks.

- Do the fast and easy items on your list first.

- As your day progresses you will find new things that you need to get done. That's okay just make sure you record your new task on the Master list. Your master list will sometimes do more growing than shrinking but don't let this discourage you. The more you find that you need to do the more you will get done.

- Draw a line thru the task when you complete the task.

- Review this list after you completing a task.

- As you review the list ask yourself this question. What the most important thing on this list that will make me the most productive and profitable? This may seem like a long question but it will keep you on track with that which is the most important thing to get done next.

- At the end of your day review what you have done. If there is something that you did but it was not on the list write it down and draw a line thru it.

- At the end of your day also review what was not completed. This will give you a head start in the next day's activities. It's always profitable to review the next day's work the night before. The practice of think about the next day's work will allow you to process the following morning with more clarity.

- Consolidate the Master list when it begins to get cluttered with too many crossed off items.

4) Using rhythm to be more productive – over time your business will flow into a natural rhythm then you will find that things make sense to get accomplished at certain times of the day, week or month. You may find that doing invoicing every Monday makes since for whatever reason. Then you know that every Monday you will be spending an allotted amount of time doing invoicing. This is often an overlooked practice in time management but by being sensitive to it will eliminate stress on your life and make you more productive and thereby more profitable.

 5) Be wise with your time – time is an asset or a liability. How we use it depends on productivity and profitability. Therefore use it wisely. Here are some tips.

-Schedule meeting in groups. If you know that you are going to be in a specific area on a particular day and you need to have a meeting then schedule it when you are going to be in that area.

- Be productive during down times. That means if you are in an area that has a potential customer drop by and drop a business card. If you find yourself waiting for a customer to give you items before your start a run then use that time to contact someone with whom you already have dropped off a business card to and see if there is any work you can do for them. Perhaps you can use this time to complete paperwork such as time sheets, invoices or develop a new sales strategy.

- Solve problems before they start a fire. If you know that you have a challenging situation developing then solve that challenge before it gets out of hand. Do you have a staff member who is not satisfying a customer? Address it before it becomes a real problem. Do you have a new run coming and you're not sure how to handle it. Then begin to interview subcontractors to do the run.

- Learn the traffic patterns. As a courier you will encounter traffic. If you know that a particular area is going to be jammed at 9am then plan an alternative route. Of course you can't avoid all traffic but think of how you can avoid the ones you know exist. Along this line of thinking when your customer gives you a run and you know that the timing is going to be a challenge because you know the traffic pattern then inform your customer and provide a reasonable solution. If they want their mail picked up at 8AM but you know they will get it quicker at 7:45AM because those 15 minutes make a difference in traffic patterns then suggest the change to your customer. They will be impressed and pleased with your insight and that you have their best interest in mind when planning a run.

Your customer's time management

As a courier you need to understand it's your customer who dictates what gets done & when it needs to get done. There will be times when you can manipulate this but even that depends on your customers. It is important that you completely understand what your customer needs and when they need it done, because they are the ones who pays your bills and keeps your business cash flow in the positive direction.

When you are in your customer's presence you are to give them your complete attention. That means if you get a personal cell phone call during this time you ignore it and allow the call to go into voice mail. Write down important items your customer is expecting and ask for clarity if you don't completely understand what is expected. Use your customer's terminology, this makes them feel like you understand them and that you can accomplish what needs to be done. When you have a meeting with your customer and the meeting is over, spend some time with small talk if your customer allows it. If the meeting is over get out of there. If you have a delivery to make, make it and get out of their place of business and onto the next thing you need to accomplish. Respect your customer's time and their staff's time. If you spend too much time wasting other peoples time then you are not being wise with your time either.

If you find yourself running late, let your customer know. We live in a culture that makes us feel like we must give a reason for everything we do. This is based on assumptions. If your customer does not ask you why you're gonna be late don't tell them. If they do ask tell them the truth. As a courier you will encounter various reasons for running late…traffic, car problems, or you have to wait for someone else to give you the work your transporting. When explaining the reason you need to be confident in your solution and reassure your customer that all is under control and that you will get there as quick as possible.

Your staff's time management

Now just as your customer's dictates your time you are the one who dictates your staff's time. Just because you dictate their time does not mean you get to waste it. The more effective your staff is with their time means they will be productive and profitable for you and for themselves. The more profitable they are the happier they will be working with you and for you.

Clearly spell out all expectations when you hire a staff member. Expectations will change over the course of time and when they do change make sure your staff is fully aware of the changes. Make sure your staff understands the time parameters for any runs or routes they do for your customers. Be fair when scheduling out their day. I once worked with a dispatch manager who insisted in giving his drivers more work than they can manage in their day. He thought that he was being a fruitful manager but all he was doing was irritating his staff and losing customers.

It is advisable that as the owner you do the runs or the routes yourself before you hand it over to someone else. That will give you a basic understanding of the challenges they may face and also give you the basic knowledge if you can get more out of your staff that they are giving you.

Check up on your staff occasionally. You can do this several ways. Give them a phone call and ask where they are and how things are going in their day. You can also be at the customers pick up or delivery locations when your driver is expected to be there. While you are there, help your staff with making the delivery. If there are boxes that need to be moved roll up your sleeves and get to work. Also, notice time of delivery and how they interact with the customer and if you see anything that needs to be address do it. Your staff and your customer will value the input.

When having conversations with your staff, keep the conversation short and to the point. There will be times when you can joke with your staff or dive into their personal life all of which is important but be wise about the timing. Don't mix too much information in the conversation. Also, avoid repeating yourself. Keep in mind that you will have certain values that will give your business a unique style over your competitors. These values need to be expressed to your staff and do that with examples both in your actions and in your words.

Chapter 12

Insurance and Bonding

The What's & Why's in Courier Service Insurance!

There are several types of insurance you will need to consider. Insurance in the courier service has changed since 9/11. Acquiring coverage has gotten harder and the price has increased over the years but it is something you will need to get in order to satisfy State requirements and obtaining customers. This chapter deals with the most basic understanding of vehicle insurance, commercial insurance, courier service insurance, reconstruction insurance, umbrella coverage for subcontractors and bonding. Insurance is a necessary evil in my option and it can become costly. But it's all the cost of doing business and thankfully it's a State and Federal taxes write off.

Basic vehicle insurance – basic vehicle insurance is mandatory in all 50 States. So you must obtain this insurance. Of course the price you pay is determined by your State's requirement as well as your personal driving record.

Commercial vehicle registration and insurance – as with basic vehicle insurance most States require commercial vehicle registration and additional vehicle insurance for the courier industry. Once again you need to contact your local vehicle registration office or your State's website to research additional coverage. Usually the additional coverage is not much more in cost than basic vehicle insurance.

Courier service insurance – there is a basic courier insurance that you should consider getting. Some States require it. Courier insurance protects against theft, loss, and damage to property in the care of the courier. No matter what you are delivering this insurance is good because it protects you from being personally liable if there is a loss of documents or items while they are in your possession. There are a number of policies you can choose from depending on the work you are doing and the cost of the items you are delivering. Grow your insurance coverage as your business grows. No need to pay for the additional insurance premium if you don't need too.

Reconstruction insurance – there will be some documents that you will carry which have valuable information on it and you will be requested by your customer to carry reconstruction insurance. This insurance will pay for the reconstruction of the information on the loss or damaged documents. The cost varies from insurance company to insurance company so it's best to shop around when you consider or need to add this type of policy to your portfolio.

Umbrella insurance coverage - as your business grows and you begin to hire sub-contractors and employees then you will need to add them to your insurance coverage. Work with your agent to ensure that the transition of adding individuals to your own umbrella policy will be smooth. Your underwriter may require additional coverage that your sub-contractor will have to carry on their own vehicle insurance. Just make sure you have a written contract that your subcontractor has signed that they will agree to the additional coverage. Along this same thought, some of your customer may ask for the same additional coverage from your subcontractors.

Surety Bonding What is surety bonding? – A surety bond is a type of insurance (it's not really insurance but a promise to pay on your behalf) that guarantees performance of a contract. If one party does not fulfill its end of the bargain, then the surety bond provides financial compensation to the other party. There are three different parties involved in a surety bond: 1) The principle (you). You and your business are being secured against defaulting on a promised service.

2) The obligee (the individual, business or company to whom you promised service too). They are being protected by financial compensation against your inability to perform services you agreed to perform.

3) The surety (insurance company or bank). This person or organization promises

to pay the obligee should the principle default. Basically, the surety assures a successful contract because it assumes all financial obligations if the principal does not deliver. If the surety pays the obligee on your behalf then you are fully responsible to repay surety.

Why do you need it? – There are several reasons why you should or need to be bonded. First of all, surety bonds establish that your company is trustworthy. When you approach a potential customer and tell them you are bonded it establishes that you are serious about your service and that you can be trusted. If your potential customer is wise about giving you're their business they will ask you if you are bonded. Secondly, bonding is required by some States for courier companies to operate within their state. You will need to check with your specific State government's rules and regulations to see if bonding is a requirement. Thirdly, there are business and companies who will not allow a courier service to acquire work unless the courier company is bonded. Fourthly, if you want to get any State or Federal contracts then you must be bonded. It is a prerequisite to the granting of receiving those contracts.

How do you get bonding? - The first step is locating a surety agent. Do a web search for bonding companies in your State. Keep in mind that you don't have to use a bonding company that's in your State. Bonding companies can acquire licenses to issue in other states beyond their State lines. The second step is for you to determine what your State's rules and regulations are in what type of surety bonding you need. Your bonding agency should have an idea. This underwriting process can unnerve you because they will ask you personal financial questions to determine if you and your business have the character and capability to perform the services you say you can perform. Start off your service with simplicity in order to acquire bonding. Another angle is to obtain the simplest form of bonding in order to satisfy State requirements and customers. As your business grows you will find that you may need to get additional bonding. But don't be concerned about that now just get the basics and grow from there.

How much bonding do you need? – The amount of bonding required will be determined by State rules and regulations. It also will be determine by the type and scope of the services you provide. And lastly, it will be determined by the amount your customer requires. Establish a healthy relationship with your agency so as your business grows they can help you in determining your bonding issues.

As you can see, insurance and bonding are requirements in the courier service. This is often the leading reason why subcontractor never branch out on their own in acquiring their own client base. Do not allow this to happen to you. Work through the issues of insurance and bonding step by step. Acquire the basics and get additional coverage as your business grows. Building a healthy relationship with your agent will go a long way. Just be careful that you don't get insurance that you don't need. Always ask the questions: Do I need this coverage? Why do I need this coverage? Can my business afford this additional grow if it's going to cost the business? Plan for growth by saving money to give your business the additional capital you need to have the right insurance at the right time. Manage your money in such a way that it's really the customer who pays for the additional insurance coverage.

Chapter 13

How to Hire & Manage Independent Subcontractors

As your business grows you will find that you will not be able to handle all of the work on your own. When this begins to happen it is time for you to hire someone to do your courier runs for you. In this line of business hiring an independent subcontractor is the way to go. It is important not to hire someone as an employee because there are all types of tax, financial & legal liabilities that go along with hiring an employee rather than an independent contractor. The number one reason is the cost savings to the company. For example, depending on the State you live in you may be required to provide benefits and pay into unemployment taxes. There will be a time when it will be wise and useful to hire an employee but at the moment let's discuss hiring and managing independent subcontractors.

Independent subcontractors, just like you, are their own courier company. What you are doing is just hiring them and their small company to do work for you and for your customers. It's very important for that relationship to be established properly right from the very start. Most of the time as your business grows; you will want to hire people that you know and trust. It is important for you to communicate to them your expectations and your customers' expectations. Always include things such as timeliness, friendliness, fostering a positive 'can do attitude'. You must create an encouraging, low stress environment for your new driver and for your customer. Here are a few suggestions when it comes to dealing with an independent subcontractor:

~ Hire someone you can trust. I suggest starting off with a family member or a friend. Hire someone who has a vested interest in your success and will care for your customers as well as you do.

~ Never send a new driver into your customers without proper training. Training should include the following:

- Personally introducing the driver to the customer.

- Walk the new driver thru every step of the process, including where they are to entire the building, who they are to see to receive the work, any documentation that needs to be signed etc... The same goes to where the driver is to deliver the work. Walk the new driver thru each step of the delivering process.

- Write all directions and expectations on a piece of paper and review this with the new driver.

- Always keep an extra copy of the directions and expectations on file. This will assist you in the future.

- Encourage proper clothing, professionalism, timeliness and positive attitude.

- Travel with the new driver for the first time. Depending on the route you may need to travel with them a couple of times to ensure confidence.

- Maintain in close contact with the new driver during the first few days of the run just to make sure all goes well. For example if they are going to be late to make it a deliver because of traffic or because of car break down they need to call you so you can inform the customer. There will be times when the driver will be tempted to by-pass you and call the customer directly but establish right from the start that the driver is to call you and allow you to best handle the situation.

- Make sure the new driver maintain their own set of records. Teach them if you have too.

~ Maintain a positive and stress free working relationship with your drivers. They are representing you and your customers. If ever you detect that something is wrong, address the issue as soon as possible. The more stress your drivers are the more likely there is to be a problem such as an accident. Do your part in reducing road rage by caring for your driver.

~ Add the driver to your umbrella insurance policy. A simple phone call is all that is needed to add your new driver to your policy. The insurance company may need additional information such as driver's name, address etc. Of course there will be an increase in your insurance premium so you will need to calculate the cost verses the benefit to expanding your company. Sooner or later if you desire to grow in your business you will have to spend the additional cost to place someone under your policy. So take the extra time to do the calculations and determine if it's the proper time to take this step.

~ Establish right from the start what you are expecting and how much you are going to pay for the service they provide. Included in this is what you're not going to pay such as parking fines and speeding tickets. Who pays for gas and tolls? Who pays for drivers errors? Etc. Keep in mind that you can't be expected to know all the incidents that may develop and nor can your new driver so it's important to develop and maintain a healthy business relationship with each independent subcontractor your hire.

~ Keep good records on your new driver. Develop a filing system that tracks what your driver does, when they do it and how much you are paying them. This will come in handy during payday and end of year taxes.

~ Pay your driver. This may seem silly to include but I have seen companies alter the day checks are received and the amount is different from the agreed price. Make sure you treat them fairly and accurately. Even if it mean you don't receive any payment yourself.

~ Do all that you can to increase the income of your driver while maintain a healthy profit. This can be done by review their work and see if there is any way you can increase their profit. For example, I had a driver that was getting stuck in traffic. I gave him an alternate route and it saved him 45 minutes in time as well as mileage, gas, and frustration. Both the driver and my customer were happier and more profitable. Also, when you collect a gas surcharge pass some of the surcharge forward to your driver. Do the same with the CPI increase. More about this later,

~ Develop your own independent subcontractor agreement. It clearly spells out in a legal form the business relationship you are developing. It may seem awkward but it serves to protect you and your driver.

Chapter 14

Payroll – Setting it up and Keeping it Running

Payroll can be confusing if you never had to keep track of it before. It's not really that hard if you follow basic setup rules right from the start when you hire an employee or an independent subcontractor. As your business grows this is often the first item that a business owner will delegate. That's fine when the time comes but at first you should learn the 'ins & outs' of payroll.

Everybody likes to get paid and everybody likes to get paid on time. Learn quickly that you don't mess around with someone else's paycheck. The best way to avoid problems is to set up a payroll system that is easy and simple. Here is a good way to set up a payroll system.

8 Steps to Setting up a Payroll System:

Step 1: Registration with State and local governmental agencies. Most States and local county agencies require you list your business in order to pay taxes. Contact your States website to determine what you need to obtain a license or a business identity number to practice doing business in the primary State that you will be conducting business. This identity number will be used to track the taxes you pay to the State. Some States will accept the EIN that is given to you by the IRS. Local governmental agencies require that you register your business at the county seat. You can visit, call or search your county's website to see what you need to do to satisfy requirements. When you contact the State revenue department you need to get a hold of a copy of IRS Circular E, as well as Publication 15-A so you can review what changes there may be in tax laws and regulations. You also need to obtain a payroll tax publication from the state your business is in.

Step 2: Acquire an employer identification number. This number is also referred to as an EIN. You get your EIN from the IRS. This number is important for reporting and paying taxes and filing other documents to the IRS and to state agencies. This number is also called the 'Employer Tax ID'. You can acquire this number directly by calling the IRS or using their website.

Step 3: Determine if your staff is an employee or an independent subcontractor. If you are hiring a driver then consider hiring them as an independent contractor. If you are hiring someone to work in your office doing accounting, bookkeeping, dispatching, sales, or another office function then you may want to consider them as an employee. The legal barrier between the two is often confusing but it's important to understand the difference because it determines who pays Federal taxes, Social Security and Medicare Taxes. It also determines if you are going to pay unemployment and State income taxes. If you hire an employee then you are required to files documentation and taxes. If you are hiring a subcontractor then they are responsible for paying State and Federal taxes. There are benefits to you and to the individual who you hire to be considered a subcontractor. Less paperwork and lower cost affect your business. However, since there is a fine line between the two it's important to determine how you are hiring this individual.

Step 4: Determine & document compensation. As discussed before, you need to determine what your staff member's work responsibilities are and determine compensation for those responsibilities. Once this is determined you should document all of this in a written agreement, signed and dated. Give allowance for alterations in the responsibilities & compensations because business will have ebbs and flows as your business grows. It's important that your new staff member understands the need to be flexible in market changes. It's important that the compensation is done in an acceptable timely manner. I know of a courier owner who would go on a one month vacation and not pay his subcontractors until he got back from vacation. This caused undue stress on the drivers. Determine the best pay period for your schedule & cash flow. As the employer you can choose whatever pay schedule suits you best based on what is most productive and most profitable for your company. The most common models for pay periods include weekly, bi-weekly, semi-monthly or monthly. But make sure that you pay your workers properly and on time.

Step 5: Keep good records. Develop a time sheet that your subcontractor driver will fill out, complete and give you at the end of the pay period. Use this time sheet to determine the amount you owe your driver. Keep this time sheet for your records. If the individual is consider an employee they must fill out the Federal Income Tax Withholding Form W-4. Your employee must complete the form and return it to you so that you can withhold the correct federal income tax from their pay. The IRS will want you to keep at least four years of all payroll payments. I suggest you never toss this information out even years after you sell your business. Once you have done the week's payroll file the documents properly under each

Step 6: Choosing your payroll system. At first you should consider manually doing your payroll for subcontractors. If you are hiring an employee then consider a basic software program. If you are at the point of hiring staff then you should be at the point of considering a payroll software program. There are many good commercial accounting software programs. Some popular options that small businesses always use to manage tax collections, direct deposits, check processing, and other such things include ADP, PayChex Online Payroll, Intuit Online Payroll, MYOB, Microsoft Money and Sage Peachtree. Ask around to some of your friends who have their own business and get their options to the features in the program they find useful.

Step 7: Doing payroll. Once you have all the information from your new staff member it's time to run payroll. You will find it helpful to set the same day of the week to run payroll. Careful review all the information on the time sheet and determine what you owe your subcontractor. Write the check and make sure you include the date of the service they provided. For example: 'Independent contractor compensation for the week of January 25 to January 30, 2014'. This is protection if you are ever audited by the IRS. Make a copy of the check and file it with the time sheet. If you are doing payroll for an employee, enter the data into the software program and the program will do all the calculations and documentation for you. Print out a copy and file it as a paperback up.

Step 8: Pay the payroll taxes. If you only hire independent subcontractors then you of course don't pay any payroll taxes. What you do have to do is tally the total payment you paid them on a 1099 which is done once a year and needs to be calculated, completed and given to your subcontractor by January 31. Give them a copy, sent a copy to the IRS, sent the State a copy and keep a copy for your records. If you hire any employees then you are to pay State and Federal taxes according to the schedule these authorities require. It may be either monthly, quarterly or annually. You can call the IRS and request the 'Employer's Tax Guide', this publications will guide you in the how & when you are to pay taxes. States also have guides to assist you in pay State taxes so be sure to call or go on their website to get a copy.

Chapter 15

Pricing your Service

Know what to charge your customer for the service you provide is determined by several factors. But before we dive into these factors we should discuss some common fallacies regarding pricing.

The first fallacy is the misunderstanding that you need to price your services below the competitor's prices. This simply is not true. Often when there is a startup company the owner or manager thinks the best way to get their foot into the door of new customers is to offer the lowest prices. Low prices may be a factor in getting new customers but that should not be the first thing you do to acquire new customers. As you have already learned there are several reasons why a potential customer will pick you over your competitor is not always the pricing. I have been in several bidding process over the years and almost all the time the lowest price did not get the work.

Once you determine what he customer values in the service they are looking for you must place yourself and your company to provide the value they are looking for. That could be several things such as timeliness, competence, reputation, billing time, general attitude of drivers, cleanliness etc…

What it really comes down to is giving your customer a fair price for the service they desire. If the price is to low the customer begins to doubt your ability, if your price is too high they will feel they are being ripped off. You need to strike a balance in your pricing. Don't underprice yourself nor undervalue yourself. Make sure to assure your customer that their pricing is not the lowest but it is the best value. Your pricing is part of your image but not your entire image.

Secondly, some people believe that pricing is a complicated endeavor. At first it may seem that way but once you do your research and your thinking you will soon be able to have enough of a structure to give a ball park pricing in a moment's notice.

Thirdly, don't panic if your competitor tries to find out your pricing nor panic if you find out they are copying your prices. Remember, you will find a market niche and provide outstanding service that will set you apart from all competition.

Fourthly, don't start your pricing calculations based on what your competition charges. This will get you in trouble. For example, I had reached out into a new area to market my services so I called local courier services to determine their prices. What I did not know was there was a price war going on between several of the local services. I had begun to give out prices for work that I knew was well below the market value. I knew this was a big mistake. Without my knowing it I became a participator in the pricing war and it nearly cost me more than I had bargain for. I soon altered course to insure success and the continuation of my business. The price war was so damaging that several courier services went out of business and I almost followed them. You need to generate a pricing structure based on several factors and those factors are… These factors are guidelines which will help you get started with your courier service business, and insure you make a profit from day one. As your business grows, you'll be able to adapt your rates to better fit the market place.

1) Determine your operations expenses. At first this may be difficult to do but it's the place to start. You need to determine how much it's going to cost you to do the run. This is to be broken down into trip expenses, daily expenses, monthly expenses and yearly expenses. Think! Sit down with paper and pen and record all the things that cost you to do the service. Maintenance, fuel and time of operation, and the number of operators and delivery personnel, all need to be taken into account. Each aspect of delivery has a price tag that a business must pay. To adequately determine the cost of operation, add the hourly wages of delivery personnel and hourly fuel and maintenance costs. Gas, tolls, phone bill, car repairs, do you use a car or a small truck, calculate insurance etc. Calculate your

operations expenses into hour segments…Once your operation expenses are calculated and known move to the next factor.

2) How much is your time worth? Bottom line to this question is how much money do you want to make for the time you have personal invested? Now, don't get greedy, be realistic. Are you satisfied with $10 an hour, $12.50 an hour, $15.00 an hour, $25.00 an hour…Combine your operation expenses into the amount of hour income you desire and this will give you a starting point to determine the charge of service.

3) Determine what other courier services are charging in your area. Make sure you are comparing apples to apples and oranges with oranges. Once you have determine your operations expense, your desired hourly rate, make a comparison with your competition will help you determine if you need to make any minor adjustments. Call the courier services in your area to check their rates. If there are several, use an average to determine a competitive rate.

4) What is the market value for your services? This can only be done if you do your research. What are people willing to pay for your services? You can't be too low and you can't be too high. Depending on where you are located will determine the market value of your services. Pricing in New York is different than in Florida. Rural areas are generally cheaper than urban areas.

5) Ask the right questions. Is the package an envelope or a case of legal papers or perhaps a van load of medical supplies? What time is the pickup in relations to traffic pattern? Is there going to be a wait time at pick up or at delivery location? Is it a rush job or is there flexibility in timing? Is the package heavy or bulky? Is it sensitive material? All these and more questions need to be asked in determining the pricing. The longer you are in this business the more you will be able to ask the right questions. Experience pays off and so do mistakes. Once you under quote a job you will never want to do that again.

6) Be ready to make pricing adjustment. There are several reasons you may have to make adjustments. You may have underestimated your overhead and find you are unable to make a decent profit at a low rate. Your competitors may have adjusted their rates. If you find that you are not getting the amount of clients you were expecting using the market strategies and sales technique laid out in this book then perhaps your prices need adjustments. If you are getting to much work then perhaps you need to raise you prices.

If you charge more than the going rate, you will probably not get many clients. The most important factor is 'what are people in your area used to and willing to pay for courier services'. In other words, you need to determine the market price.

7) Simplify your pricing to an hourly rate. Once you have been able to do all your calculations then develop an hourly rate will enable you to quickly give price quotes over the phone once you have determine how long it will take to do a particular run. Keep in mind all the other factors when determining how long it will take to do a run. Like loading and unloading time, wait time, traffic issues etc.

8) Don't forget…wait time, holiday seasons, weekend rates, night rates, gas surcharges etc. when determining pricing.

These several strategies will ensure your competitiveness, happiness, and overall business success. If you're starting a courier service business, figuring out what to charge for each delivery job can be a challenge. You don't want to overbid and lose potential new customers.

Chapter 16

Generating Extra Income Growth

There are ways to increase income growth with your current customers. Increasing the prices on customers is always a gamble. If you increase prices will your customer begin to give their business to another courier company? There will be times when you will not be able to increase prices but instead decrease them to keep a customer. However, there are three ways in which you can increase your revenue with your customers.

Gas price increases - There are several areas where I suggest you entertain the thought of price increases. The first is when gasoline prices begin to increase. I have developed a gas matrix for my customers. This matrix clarifies for the customers what they will be paying as gas prices increase. The matrix calculates a percentage surcharge when the price of gasoline is between certain dollar amounts. This surcharge is added to the invoice between the sub total and the total. This is a simple uncomplicated method to protect your profits when gas prices flux.

When I first implemented the gas matrix a few customers argued the price increase. It was simply a manner of explaining to the customer that as gas prices increases you have no choice but to do a modest price adjustment and that as soon as prices decrease so will the surcharge. Keep in mind that you don't want to lose a customer over a gas surcharge and I'm pleased that I have never lost a customer due to the surcharge. If you face increase opposition handle each customer separately and customize a gas surcharge that is acceptable. Gas prices have their ups and downs and the matrix clarifies for your customer what they will be paying as the prices flux. A sympathetic customer will clearly understand that this is something that affects every single American who utilizes a vehicle.

Consumer Price Index (CPI) - another opportunity to increase prices is using the yearly consumer price index. Every year the federal government sends out a percentage point (usually February) which tells how much consumer prices have increased over the past year. The Federal government's report is useful. You can access this report via the internet. Do internets searches for 'Consumer Price Index' and you will find links to the government's report.

This report does an outstanding job in covering all areas of consumer spending. You can utilize the transportation increase however that number can be rather high. There are also regional reports such as northeast or southwest areas of the USA. The government takes numbers from all the consumer price adjustment and averages them out to certain overall percentage. This is the number I use because it's an easy number to justify a price increase. I have never had a customer argue a price increase which was based on the CPI. By using the CPI your customers will find a price increase to be fair and accurate throughout economic situation in our nation. Not only will your customers find this type of increase to be fair, but you will find it helpful because it keeps your business growing at the same rate as our nation's economic situation alters. There is a direct correlation between your growth and your expenses.

Alteration in runs – From time to time a customer will want to add stops or additional work to an already existing run. This is an opportunity to increase your profit. There are times when you can do a run for a customer for free. Do this as long as it's in your best interest. If it does not cost you anything then you can chose to toss your customer a freebie. This will help build a stronger relationship with your customer. However, if the extra work is regular and will cost you in time, energy, effort or money then use the extra work to increase your profits.

Wait time – There will be times when you get to a customer at the agreed time but the package is not ready for you to pick up. This situation happens and you need to be ready for it. Waiting for a package slows down momentum, puts you off schedule and can generate frustration. To help in offsetting this you need to charge the customer wait time. Once you have determine your hourly rate (See Chapter 15) than you can divide wait time into 15 minute segments, 10 minute segments, or five minute segments. If you have to wait under 5 minutes, no surcharge but once you have to wait longer than five minutes start the clock. Trust me, if you don't start charging for wait time the customer will begin to take advantage of your generosity.

Heavy or bulky Packages – charge more for heavy packages. You can do this by charging an extra dollar per pound. Bulky packages my not weigh a lot but they consume a large area to transport. You decide if you want to charge extra for this but if it cuts into your ability to do other work than you must charge extra.

Rush orders & after-hours orders – this is an area of extra income, especially if you are will to pay the price. Rush deliveries can cost you more in gas and the chance of traffic tickets increase. If you are will to work longer days then the extra cash rolls in when you do after-hours services. At the outset consider working 24/7. Once your business is up and running you can hire other drivers to ease the pressure. Just make sure you charge enough to pay another individual.

Warehousing and Record storage – You will quickly learn that your customers have other needs such as storing documents, equipment and other items that they need but do not want at their site. After some research and minimal investment you will be able to provide this type of service. Don't jump into this type of business until you have mastered the courier service.

Chapter 17

Billing Customers and Collecting Payment

When approaching a potential individual, business or company about gaining them as customers there are many things that must be thought about. One of the important things that must be thought about and discussed is the billing process and payment. You of course are excited to receive a new customer but don't take on a customers who you understand will be difficult to collect payment from for the outstanding service you provide.

At this juncture we will assume that there was an agreement between you and your new customer regarding service and payment amount, so let's review how you bill and collect payment. To some this may sound simple but be warned....many of businesses has failed because of billing errors and insufficient payment for services provided.

1. Establish the billing cycle with customer. What is a billing cycle? A billing cycle is the time and payment arrangement between services provided and payment of those services. This is something that you want to control. Keep in mind that there will be companies who dictate the billing cycle rules and you have no choice but to comply. But it is in your best financial and business success to control the rules that dictate billing cycle.

2. Keep the billing cycle short. Do not allow a length time period between services rendered and payment received. The ideal situation is for you to provide services for a week, than bill for that service at the end of the week and collect payment the following week. This is efficient to your cash flow. Even if you are only doing one run a week for your customer it is ideal if you make arrangements to bill and collect within a two week period.

3. Do not accept payment arrangements that go beyond a 30 day cycle. Cash flow is the fuel to your business. Literally! Without the proper cash flow you will be limited in the expansion of your new venture. Cash flow is the

movement of money as it goes out (fuel, insurance, advertising, and payroll) and as it comes in (billable). A 30 day billing cycle makes cash flow predictable and profitable.

4. Be efficient in billing customers. If you send out billing in an unorganized and untimely fashion expect trouble. Avoid trouble…do your work and bill your customer properly.

~This means as soon as you can send out an invoice according to the arrangements with your customer do it.

~ Use a simple and understandable bill. This avoids confusion.

~Don't make any mistakes in the billing. Mistakes are monkeys' wrenches in the billing cycle which means a limitation to your cash flow which you could have avoided.

~ Be consistent in the format of the invoice and in the timing your customer receives the invoice. Somewhere in your customer's accounts payable department is an individual who likes order and respect timeliness. Give them what they want so you can get what you want.

5. Get the bill into the hands of the individual who writes the check. Even if it means you hand delivers the bill directly. I love this approach because it gives you the ability to establish a healthy relationship with the person who affects your cash flow. It also allows you the ability to detect any challenges that you may encounter as you collect funds. For example, you may learn that this individual is leaving on a two week vacation. This will affect the billing cycle and it gives you time to plan accordingly.

6. Keep mindful of the billing cycle. Don't lose tract of when you are to receive payment because the longer the payment exceeds the agreeable billing cycle the harder it is to collect the payment.

7. Establish a late fee for overdue payment. Whatever the payment timing arrangements are there is to be a time limit to the credit you are extending

to your customer. A good guideline is 50% of the billing cycle. Calculate 50% of the days the billing cycle is due then any days over that you are to charge a late fee. For example, if you are to receive payment within 30 days and you do not receive payment within those 30 days than you are to charge a fee if you do not receive payment within the next 15 days. Do not charge anything less than 10% of the billable. Accountants hate paying late fees and will do what they can to construct an accounts payable that will not accrue a late fee.

8. Passionately and properly collect accounts receivables when your customer is not paying accordingly to the billing cycle. Here is how you are to be passionate and proper.

~When the payment is outside the terms call (proper) the customer and let them gently know that you have not receive payment yet (passion). Give your customer the benefit of any doubt that they are making the payment in a timely fashion but for some reason there was a glitch in the system beyond your customer's ability.

~Follow up with the customer when you still don't receive payment (passion). Ask to speak with the individual who is responsible for accounts payable (proper). Use this time to remind customer that they are approaching the late fee deadline and the late fee will be added to the next invoice (passion). Don't threaten or demand (proper).

~ Stay on top of the customer (passion). Call them every day if you have too. Include mailing them a reminder note. And with each contact increase the demand for the payment (proper). Inform them that lack of payment affects the ability you have in properly servicing them and other customers.

~ If you still don't receive payment within an acceptable time frame inform customer that you will stop doing work for them (passion and proper). In today's business climate the customer is highly valued and rightfully so. However, a better understanding is that a paying customer is highly valued.

~ The last course of action is to stop doing work for the customer and take them to court to receive your just due payment. Include all billable work, late fees, lawyer fees, court fees and business cost that it took to collect funds. Of course this is the last course of action but necessary in order for you function properly and profitably. This will be a challenge to you but this will demonstrate your resolve to do the things necessary for you to function in today's competitive market. It's never right to do work for someone who does not pay according to terms in a timely fashion.

Chapter 18

Smart Phones & Useful Computer Software

Once you have handed out your business card you must become available to your customers and potential customers. And may I add 24/7! The best means is a cell phone. Cell phone technology has become a valuable business tool. There are many styles and options for phone service available but there are several features you will find extremely important.

Cell phone – When I started in the courier service the best technology was beepers. The customer would beep me and I would find the nearest pay phone and return the call to the customer. The development of the cell phone made life simpler for me, my drivers and my customers. Cell phones have become a valuable tool. It's important to back up your information stored on your cell phone. This can be done the old fashion way as in a notebook or utilizing a computer to back up your files. As technologies increase you will find investing in a smart phone to be helpful. Become familiar with the all the features your phone provides and use all of them.

Just like your business cards…always keep your cell phone with you. Make sure you keep it charged by investing in a car phone charger. Also, keep an eye on up and coming smart phone application programs and updates.

Voice mail – Allowing your customers call to go into voice mail is helpful. There will be times when you simply will not be able to take the call. Once you retrieve the message call your customer back and let them know you have received the message. This places them at easy that you are addressing their concern quickly.

Email – Many phone services provides email. E-mail capability is very handy especially when you are on the road. Some customers, once they know your email, will rather give you information via email. There have been times when a customer calls me to give me an address or contact information and I have asked them to email me the information. This allows me freedom and insures accurate information. This is useful for a number of reasons: accurate information, safety while on the road, its instantaneous, I can review the material at any time and make correct decisions that will satisfy a customer's request.

Contact files - Investing a few moments to program your customers information into your smart phone provides you with information simply by tapping a few buttons. Contact information is great because at the push of a few buttons you will gain all the information that you've already programmed into your cell phone regarding your customer. Whenever you get a customer even a potential customer always take a few moments and enter their data into your cell phone. Those few minutes of entering that data will be very useful. It's time-saving and will turn into a money making opportunities in the years to come. I have found some of this information that you can put into your contact to be overburdening but the nice thing is that there is so much information that you can store it's almost seems endless.

GPS features – When you need quick directions from one location to another or simply need an alternative route the GPS feature will save you energy, time and perhaps embarrassment. As your business develops you will need to invest in a mapping software program but we will cover that topic in another area. Some smart phones that have GPS technology built-in also have other applications such as Google. I have used this technologies countless times. It is particularly helpful in determining traffic patterns and also detouring around particular problems.

Internet access – The whole world lies at your fingertips and you can learn so much about your potential customer and even keep an eye on your competition. I have found the online 'White and Yellow Pages' useful while on the road.

110

Smart phone apps – smart phone are great because there are all sorts of applications that directly impact your productivity and profitability. Here are a few apps that you will find useful…keep in mind there are new apps be developed what seems to be daily, so be prepared to grow with the technology. Beat the Traffic, G-Park, Gas buddy, MapQuest, Tracking device, My Park Pro, Trapster, iWrecked, Repair Pal, Accufuel, Greenmeter, Car finder, Evernote, eOffice, google.com/voice, accuweather.com, and my personal favorite Pandora

Business Contact software – This is important software. At first you can keep this information in a notebook but you will soon learn that having contact information in an electronic format will be valuable and useful. Especially when you can upload or download contact information into a smart phone and take the information with you.

This software manages all types of information including but not limited to Company name, address, phone number, fax number, cell phone numbers, email address, website address and the specific information that pertains to key individuals within your customer's organization. There are often areas where you can enter in birthdays, anniversaries, children's birthday etc…

It is helpful to maintain a notebook that has the same information that you place into the contact program. Whenever I add a new contact into electronically form, I print out the information and insert it into the notebook. Which I keep with me at all times.

The most useful software have the ability to setup on your laptop or desktop computers programming that make the information available to you with a single click of a button. From this programming you can receive reminders of important time and dates. Launch into other programs that give you needed services such as letter writing, emailing, phone calling and internet browsing.

Intergrading software package - Consider buying an intergrading software package. Intergrading software often includes business contacts, a spreadsheet program, a word processing program, web page program, graphics program, journaling program and/or a publishing program. They are expensive and not all software is alike. Stick with a company, although costly, who has the reputation for integration of different software programs and available updates. I'm partial to Microsoft products because it's what I started with and have become efficient in using. Before lying out the big bucks for an integrated software system consider the timing and growth of your business. But no matter how large you grow you will find this technology time saving and helpful in managing your business.

Mapping program – Microsoft, DeLorme and Google all have mapping software with GPS connection. Having a mapping program which uses GPS service is a wonderful new technological tool which is extremely valuable to a courier company. These software systems can be utilized to calculate out a courier route. I personally prefer DeLorme which is a software program that you enter in a starting point and ending point, then various stop points along the way. The various stop points can be programmed from point to point or simply enter all the locations and the program will calculate the most cost effective and time saving route.

This is useful when you have a customer who is requiring you to pick up at a particular location and make several deliveries with a final destination in mind. This software is also helpful with sales because it has in it a business directory of the entire United States, which includes company name, address and phone number. I suggest loading up this valuable tool to your laptop computer because if you are on the road and you have some down time you can research potential new customers.

Accounting software program - as your company grows you will need to invest in some sort of accounting software program such as Quicken books. You can set up the software to assist you in your daily income and expenses. It is also a helpful tool in assisting you in calculation tax information. As your business grows the software also helps you establish accurate record keeping for your independent contractors. We will talk more about how you hire independent contractors and how to manage them. So for the moment as your business starts you will find it helpful to start using an accounting program that way your knowledge of the program will grow as your company grows. You do not need this accounting software program to start your company but as your business grows you most certainly will want to add this valuable tool.

Billing software – you will find that many accounting software programs have the capabilities to generate invoices. If you are starting out I recommend using a spreadsheet like 'Excel'. It does not take long to learn how to use the program and you can customize the invoice to look the way you want. Once programmed it's very easy generate invoices at the click of a few buttons. Always print out an additional copy to keep in your files. This will be useful in keeping track of your customer's payments, more about how to billing and record keeping in a later chapter. Don't forget to add your logo in the invoice.

Computers – of course all of this technology means that at some point in your venture you will need a computer. Desk top computers are nice and you will want to invest in one. However, starting out I highly recommend a laptop computer. The cost has greatly reduced over the years and their durability is outstanding.

Laptops – You will find that a laptop will benefit you and your business. Laptop cost range from a couple of hundred dollars to a few thousand. Stick to the basics at first, but keep in mind that you want a computer that will be able to handle several software programs that consume large amounts of computer memory. Mapping programs, intergraded office programs, accounting

113

programs and record keeping all need a large working hardware system. So start off with a laptop that will be able to handle your personal and business growth. Laptops are portable and this makes them very useful to you.

I placed a laptop mounted in my car. There are frames which mount between your driver's seat and your passenger's seat in your vehicle. The cost is about $100.00 and if you are fairly handy you can install this unit yourself. Once you are able to invest in this setup you will love it. This will greatly increase your efficiency and therefore you're productive which leads to more profitability. Once you become proficient in your software programs you will be able to save a tremendous amount of time.

Along with this – there are two must haves as your business grows. One is a portable hard drive. Use this to back up you customer files; invoicing etc. the second item is an internet 'hot spot'. This is a mobile internet access unit these will allow you to use the internet while on the road. This can be costly but if you need to gain internet access without having to spot at a free Wi-Fi location then this hot spot will be profitable.

These items are helpful but costly so don't rush out and start buying these items or service until your company is productive and profitable. Be wise in your growth.

Chapter 19

Business Website

In today's business world you must have a website. At first you may defer the decision to have a web presence because of cost but keep in mind that as your business grows and your are generating enough income to set up a website do so. A website will offer you several things.

First, it establishes your legitimacy as a business. Customer and potential customers have quick access to the internet and they will do a business search of you and your business. If you don't have a website eventual it will cast a shadow on your ability as a businessman or woman. . Most people just assume that you have a website since the vast majority of small businesses do. If you don't have a website you will be encouraging your customers and potential customers to shop elsewhere. If you want your business to be taken seriously then get a website. You don't want to establish this reputation because it will be hard to change and it will lose you customers. Your website will quickly build trust and credibility.

Secondly, it will get you new customers. Often, when an individual, business or company needs courier service they will do a search via the internet. Don't miss out on the potential of reaching new customers. Any business that does not have a website is missing out on one of the most powerful marketing tools available. A website will give the impression that youa re bigger and more successful that you may actually be. This is a great thing about the internet, the size of your company does not matter.

Thirdly, it communicates to your competitors that you are a force to be reckoned with. This will work in your favor when you are expanding your business or when you desire to build a relationship with another courier service. You will be surprised to find that may of your competitors do not have a website. This gives you a competitive edge in legitimacy and attracting new business. By having a good website you will win clients away from your competitors - Many of your competitors will have older, home-made or badly designed websites. This will affect their credibility and search engine rankings. A well designed and engaging small business website will make you a more credible option and will also list you well above these competitors.

Fourthly, websites are inexpensive and are easy to establish. The startup cost is about $400.00 to $500.00 a year which will includes a domain name registration. Most website hosting sites provide step by step instructions in web design and construction. If you are personally not skilled in setup up a website then I'm sure you have a friend or know someone who could setup the website for you at a low cost. If you are on a tight budget you can even get free websites. Remember you don't need a giant ten thousand page website for your business; just a simple site that tells people about your company and your service is all that is needed.

Website Tips

Keep it simple but cast a large presence. I have seen website of large multinational companies that have a simple website. They are not bogged down with an overabundance of useless information. And yet at the same time you want your website to give your courier service the image that you are large and competent. Even if it's only you who does the deliveries you want your website to make you look large than what you actually are. An efficient website with good navigation and accessible content, will allow you to compete more effectively with many of your larger competitors. Keep in mind that you don't want to make promises that you can't keep but you want to give communicate that you can and will do what they need.

Keep the site clean and professional – I have seen websites that were busy with odd colors, crazy fonts and poor layout. You don't need a lot of information on the website. Cast your image, your ability and keep contact information simple and on the first page. Don't have your site uneasy to get information. Most business people are busy so they don't take the time to click through a lot of pages to get the information they want. A quality website equals a quality business. This perception will give you potential clients. A business that invests in a quality website demonstrates its commitment to providing a quality service.

Communicate the values you know your customers value – timeliness, insurance and bonding, confidentiality, cost effectiveness, ability to move an envelope, small packages, to multitude of boxes. Include your ability to work around the clock and go where they need you to go. Anticipate your potential clients' needs. You would be surprised how often a potential clients is lost because they can't find a telephone number or contact email, or any number of other basic, essential pieces of information such as; business location and how to find, opening / service times etc. Provide the essential information your potential clients need and they will take you seriously.

Know the basics of SEO (Search Engine Optimization) - Your website won't do you as much good if no one can stumble upon it. Become familiar with the SEO basics to make it more accessible by search engine. SEO can become a complex science but you should become away how search engines work and how to get you company's website on the first page of search engine results. If you do not know how to optimize your website than consider hiring an individual who can assist you, but be careful not to get rip-off. Network among you family, and friends in finding someone who has the skill set. Most of the time it's simply a matter of making sure your website is coded correctly. There is no reason that you can't get your site to rank in Google ahead of your competitor and siphon off some of their traffic. This is a big part of the reason that a website is even more important for a small business than a big one, it tends to level the playing field. Attract new clients with high and 'accurate' search engine listings.

117

Suggested website hosting Companies

Here are ten website hosting that are perfect to start your website. I have used several of these companies and you will find that they are helpful in assisting you in building your own website. When you are ready to start your website, review each of these companies and determine which is right for you. Because of their competitiveness the prices are cheap and they provide all the tools, even for beginners to build their own website. Through them you can buy your domain name. They will monitor the business of yearly domain service for you. Cost for they hosting your website can be as low as a $1.00 a month. Be careful to not get trapped into paying for services that at first you will not need. As your company grows there may be some features they offer which will be of benefit for you. The goal is to get your business an internet face.

iPage – www.ipage.com

justhost.com – www.justhost.com

web.com – www.web.com

network solutions – www.networksolutions.com

bluehost- www.bluehost.com

hostgator- www.hostgator.com

1&1- www.1and1.com

Fatcow- www.fatcow.com

Hub- www.hub.com

GoDaddy –www.godaddy.com

Chapter 20

Vehicle Care and Fleet Management

The type of vehicle you have will depend on what type of courier service you desire to do. This can range from a bike to a small truck. The majority of courier services started with a small car and expanded their vehicles depending on how they grew their business. Since cars are used mostly it would only be wise to discuss what vehicles are ideal to start with and how to care properly for your car in order to increase the longevity of your vehicle and increase your profitability.

Types of vehicles – if you are just starting and don't have the choice at the moment go out and buy a vehicle than start with the one that you have and get the most out of it. But keep in mind that whatever vehicle you start with will not and should not limit you or your business. As you progress in the market place you will discover that there is a large range of vehicles in the courier industry. And your goal in getting started is to match (market) the type of work you do with your vehicle and expand as your market expands. No matter what your vehicle you have, keep the following information in mind when dealing with this aspect of your business.

Vehicle cleanliness – Keep your vehicle clean on the inside and on the outside. Your vehicle represents you and your business. So it is important to have a clean car. Wash your vehicle every two weeks if it looks like it needs washing or not. And of course more if you find that the areas you need to work are dirtying your car more quickly. If you live in an area where there is snow fall and salt is used to deice roads then make sure you use a car washing service that washes the undercarriage of your car. Salt is deadly on vehicles, eating at rubber, plastics and metal parts.

Since you will be in your vehicles most of the day it's easy to allow trash to build up in your car. Trash such as food wrappings, discarded notes, reading material, clothing, coffee cups and anything else you happen to acquire during the working day. Clean out your car every day. Believe it or not this will help you become a better courier and a better courier is a profitable courier. I had an independent contractor who, unknown to me, was not keeping the inside of his vehicle clean. One day he went to a bank and picked up their daily checks. He had several bank pick-ups on his route and at the end of his route he had accumulated seven bags of checks. When he went to drop off the bags of checks at the main office he only had six. He double checked his car and because of the trash he allowed to accumulate, it took him over twenty minutes to find the bag. And that was after I started to help him look for the missing bag in his car. Keeping your car clean from unwanted waste will help you find missing items and keep you from embarrassing moments if not a financial penalty.

Road tools – Make sure you have your basic vehicle tools. Items such as jumper cables, jack, flashlight, lug nut wrench and extra fuses. It would be wise to also travel with a bag of tools such as wrenches, sockets, hammer and screwdrivers. And by all means, keep an extra key in a magnet box some where you can easily get too when you accidentally lock yourself out of your car.

I once had a worker who even stored extra car parts in his car. Like water pump and fuel filter. He worked for me for several years and one day I asked him how come I never had to assist him in his vehicle break downs. His reply was 'I maintain my car and I carry extra parts if I think I might need it soon'. He proceed to tell me that one day his water pump broke so he pulled over and replaced it right on the side of the road. I know it sounds extreme but his attitude kept him on the road and earned him a healthy income. I know that every courier does not have the temperament or the skills to do what he did but if you stretch yourself you can save yourself time and money. This skill will come in handy when you start hiring other drivers and your fleet starts to grow.

Road service – get a road service agreement. Your insurance company and companies like AAA offer road service. They are inexpensive considering how they can save you money, convenience and time. All you need to do is make a phone call, give them your location and they will be out to assist you. It could be a simple battery jump, gas or a tow to the nearest service station or to your home or mechanic.

Weekly vehicle maintenance – there are several things you should do on a weekly bases to insure your vehicle stays road ready. Check the fluids like oil level, radiator fluid, windshield washer fluid, power steering fluid and brake fluid. In order to get the best gas mileage, check the air pressure in your tires. Give our vehicle a general inspection and try to avoid any potential problem.

Monthly vehicle maintenance – change your oil every 5,000 miles. Check your brake pads and tires for any signs of wear. Check your transmission fluid level and notice any discoloration. If there are any signs that the vehicle needs special attention don't neglect the signs. You can do the work yourself or hire a mechanic. Speaking of which…

Find a good, trustworthy mechanic – when you lack the skills to maintain your vehicle or fix it yourself then its good for your business and your customers to find a mechanic with whom you can build a health relationship. Let the mechanic know what you use the vehicle for and that when you need it serviced you need the work to be completed in a timely manner. Good mechanic will hear what you are saying and provide quality service in a timely manner because you will in return provide them with other work when you need it done.

Expect to get all you can out of your vehicle – it will not take long before the mileage adds up on your vehicle. Don't worry…if you take care of your vehicle your vehicle will take care of you. I had an individual who worked for me got 500,000 miles out of his small cargo van before he replaced the engine. It's been years since I have heard from him but the last I heard he was doing a six hour daily run on the PA Turnpike racking up the miles in his new engine. He took care of his vehicle and his vehicle was taking care of him…that run was earning him about $1200.00 a week. I had another coworker who also reached the half million mile marker in his car. He was meticulous in caring for his vehicle and it paid off.

Expect to get more out of your vehicle but only if you care and maintain your vehicle.

Rental car service – find a local car rental place which also rents cargo vans. Build a relationship with this local business, it will come in handy. Of course there may be moments when you need to rent a car to use while yours is in the shop but you will also find the need to rent a cargo van or a small cube truck when your customers need something extra moved. You will learn that with a healthy business relationship with this rental company they will do all they can to provide you with what you need, when you need it and at the lowest possible price.

Vehicle registration – depending on the State you work in there may be a special vehicle registration you need to perform the services you do for your customer. You may be able to get away with no special registration and that would be great but some States require commercial tags for your vehicle if you use your vehicle for business. Double check your State requirements. You can get this information at a local registration office or on the States website.

Vehicle insurance – do what you can to keep your insurance premiums low. But do so with adequate vehicle insurance coverage. There are a lot of variables when it comes to vehicle insurance. Personal driving record, mileage to work, mileage while at work, and type of vehicle are only a few to mention. As always it's best to find an insurance agency that can provide all the insurance you need and be flexible enough to handle the growth of your business. The discussion of business insurance is dealt with in another chapter. But if you're able to find an agency to handle all aspect of your insurance needs you will find that there is often a health discount on the policies you need to have to cover all your business needs.

Fleet management – in time you will see your business growing and you will have to decide how best to react according to the growth. By now you have develop your niche in the courier service industry. You have seen how your competitors do business, you have interacted with enough customers to have a good handle on how to open new doors and you have grown not only personally but also financially. But now you find yourself in the position to expand your fleet of vehicles. What do you do?

First of all, diversify your independent subcontractors. Hire part time drivers with vans or specialized vehicles to handle your customers.

Secondly, rent vehicles for a short time as the new work requires a new vehicle. This may seem costly in the long run but it will help you get over a vehicle crisis in the short run thus maintaining cash flow.

Thirdly, go out and buy what you need. If you need a new small economical car, go get one. If you need a small cargo van, go get one. If you need a large cargo van, go get one. If you are expanding in transporting people go get a luxury car or SUV. Be smart and get what you need to make your business grow and keep your customers happy.

Chapter 21

Closing Comments

You have all you need to start and manage your own courier service. Now the rest is up to you. As you start and manage your focus should be on one thing....growth, growth and more growth. Grow professionally, financially and personally. There will be times of shrinkage and setbacks but keep your eye on the target and grow a company with outstanding service and excellence and you will have a business which will take care of you and your family for years to come.

There is so much to learn as a business grows and you will need to be diligent in preparing yourself for the growth. Read, learn and work to apply what you have learned to your business and you will reap the great rewards. God Bless.

45090606R00072

Made in the USA
Middletown, DE
24 June 2017